# THE 100+ SERIES™

# READING COMPREHENSION

**Essential Practice for Advanced Reading Comprehension Topics**

## Grade 4

Carson-Dellosa Publishing LLC
Greensboro, North Carolina

**Credits**
Content Editor: Erin McCarthy
Proofreader: Carrie D'Ascoli

Visit *carsondellosa.com* for correlations to Common Core, state, national, and Canadian provincial standards.

Carson-Dellosa Publishing LLC
PO Box 35665
Greensboro, NC 27425 USA
carsondellosa.com

ISBN 978-1-4838-1562-6
07-311227784

# Table of Contents

Table of Contents/Introduction............... 3

Common Core Alignment Chart ............. 4

Main Idea ................................. 5

Identifying Details......................... 16

Summarizing.............................. 31

Reading for Information.................... 36

Sequencing............................... 40

Compare and Contrast .................... 41

Cause and Effect ......................... 48

Fact or Opinion........................... 54

Classifying ............................... 59

Author's Purpose ......................... 63

Author's Viewpoint ....................... 69

Inference ................................. 76

Predicting................................. 85

Reference ................................ 86

Context Clues............................. 88

Figure of Speech ......................... 89

Vocabulary............................... 92

Genre .................................... 99

Poetry .................................. 101

Story Elements: Character ............... 103

Story Elements: Setting ................. 107

Story Elements: Mixed .................. 109

Interpreting Information................... 114

Answer Key ............................. 120

# Introduction

Organized by specific reading skills, this book is designed to enhance students' reading comprehension. The engaging topics provide meaningful and focused practice. The reading passages are presented in a variety of genres, including fiction, nonfiction, and poetry. Subject matter from across the curriculum, including topics from science, history, and literary classics, deepens student knowledge while strengthening reading skills.

The grade-appropriate selections in this series are an asset to any reading program. Various reading skills and concepts are reinforced throughout the book through activities that align to the Common Core State Standards in English language arts. To view these standards, please see the Common Core Alignment Chart on page 4.

# Common Core Alignment Chart

| Common Core State Standards* | | Practice Page(s) |
|---|---|---|
| **Reading Standards for Literature** | | |
| Key Ideas and Details | 4.RL.1–4.RL.3 | 14, 15, 20–23, 33, 42, 50, 51, 56, 60, 61, 69–76, 78–81, 85, 89, 100, 102–110, 112–114, 117, 119 |
| Craft and Structure | 4.RL.4–4.RL.6 | 69, 70, 74, 75, 85, 92, 103 |
| Integration of Knowledge and Ideas | 4.RL.7–4.RL.9 | 42, 71, 114, 119 |
| Range of Reading and Level of Text Complexity | 4.RL.10 | 14, 15, 20–23, 33, 42, 50, 51, 56, 60, 61, 69–76, 78–81, 102–110, 112, 113, 117 |
| **Reading Standards for Informational Text** | | |
| Key Ideas and Details | 4.RI.1–4.RI.3 | 5–13, 16–19; 24–32, 34–41, 43–49, 52–55, 57–59, 62–68, 77, 82–84, 86, 87, 94, 96, 97, 99, 101, 111, 115, 116, 118 |
| Craft and Structure | 4.RI.4–4.RI.6 | 17, 18, 24–27, 34–35, 40, 44–49, 52, 53, 59, 64, 65, 82, 83, 86, 87, 94, 111 |
| Integration of Knowledge and Ideas | 4.RI.7–4.RI.9 | 24, 25, 28, 29, 62–65, 68, 115–118 |
| Range of Reading and Level of Text Complexity | 4.RI.10 | 5–13, 16–19, 24–27, 30–41, 43–49, 52–55, 57, 59, 62–63, 66–68, 77, 82–84, 86, 87, 96, 97, 99–101, 115, 116, 118 |
| **Writing Standards** | | |
| Text Types and Purposes | 4.W.1–4.W.3 | 28, 29 |
| Range of Writing | 4.W.10 | 28, 29 |
| **Language Standards** | | |
| Vocabulary Acquisition and Use | 4.L.4–4.L.6 | 86–93, 94, 95, 97, 98, 101, 102, 104, 105 |

Read the passage. Then, complete the activity.

# Insects in Winter

In the summertime, insects can be seen buzzing and fluttering around us. But as winter's cold weather begins, the insects seem to disappear. Do you know where they go? Many insects find a warm place to spend the winter.

Ants try to dig deep into the ground. Some beetles stack up in piles under rocks or dead leaves.

Female grasshoppers don't even stay around for winter. In autumn, they lay their eggs and die. The eggs hatch in the spring.

Bees also try to protect themselves from the winter cold. Honeybees gather in a ball in the middle of their hive. The bees stay in this tight ball trying to stay warm.

Winter is very hard for insects, but each spring the survivors come out, and the buzzing and fluttering begins again.

1. Use the passage to complete the topic sentence below. Fill in the rest of the ovals with supporting details.

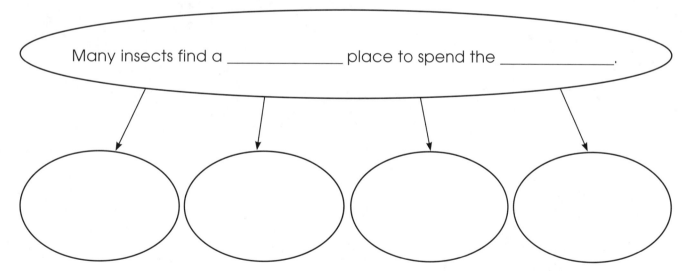

Many insects find a _____ place to spend the _____.

Read the passage. Then, complete the activity.

# Pompeii

   Almost 2,000 years ago, Pompeii was a rich and beautiful city in the Bay of Naples. The city lay close to a great volcano, Mount Vesuvius.

   One day, Vesuvius began to rumble and erupt. Lava, steam, and ash burst from the volcano. Soon, the sky was black with ash. The ash rained down on Pompeii. The people tried to hide in buildings or escape to the sea in boats. But, the ash fell so quickly that people were buried wherever they were. The city was covered with over 12 feet (3.5m) of ash.

   In recent years, scientists have found Pompeii. Much of its contents were just as they were the day Mount Vesuvius erupted. This discovery has helped us learn more about ancient Roman times.

1.  Using the details from the passage, fill in each column on the chart. Summarize information about Pompeii before, during, and after the eruption.

| Pompeii before the Eruption | Pompeii during the Eruption | Pompeii after the Eruption |
|---|---|---|
| | | |

Read the passage. Then, answer the questions.

# Dyes

Can you imagine how dull everything around you would seem without color? Dye is a substance that gives color to many things. For over 5,000 years, people have used dyes. Until the mid-1800s, only natural dyes were used. These dyes came from different parts of plants, such as the bark, roots, berries, or flowers. Certain plants produce certain colors. The indigo plant produces a blue dye. The madder plant produces bright red and brown dyes. The bark and leaves of oak, maple, and walnut trees were used to make yellow, orange, and black dyes.

In 1856, an 18-year-old boy in England discovered how to make dyes from chemicals. Chemical dyes are **synthetic**. This means that they are manufactured, not natural. Today, almost all dyes are synthetic. Synthetic dyes are made in thousands of beautiful shades.

1. The two major types of dyes that have been used are _____.

    A. indigo and liquid

    B. chemical and synthetic

    C. natural and synthetic

    D. roots and berries

2. Dyes made with chemicals were discovered in the year _____.

    A. 1856

    B. 1800

    C. 1922

    D. 500

3. Which of the following is the best topic sentence for the first paragraph?

    A. Without color, everything would seem dull.

    B. For thousands of years, people used natural dyes.

    C. The madder plant makes red and brown dyes.

    D. The indigo plant produces a blue dye.

4. Dyes that are made from chemicals are _____.

    A. natural

    B. shades

    C. liquid

    D. synthetic

Read the passage. Then, answer the questions on page 9.

# Marco Polo

It is difficult to imagine what the world was like in 1254. Europe was living in an age that we call the Medieval Period. It was a time of castles, knights and nobles, swords and lances, and many wars.

During that time, Marco Polo was born in Venice, Italy. Life in Venice was different from life in most of Europe. Venice was a city of beautiful buildings and water canals. Many merchants brought riches from other countries to trade in Venice. Marco Polo's father and uncle were merchants. They had traveled to a far-off country called Cathay. (Cathay is now called China.) There, they had become friends with the great ruler, Kublai Khan. He invited them to return.

When Marco Polo was 17 years old, he began a journey to China with his father and uncle. They sailed the Indian Ocean and crossed the deserts and mountains of Asia on camels. The journey to China took three years.

Kublai Khan greeted the Polos and showered them with gifts. He was especially impressed with Marco, who could speak four languages.

Khan sent Marco on many trips through China. On these trips, Marco saw many amazing things that he had never seen in Europe, such as coal used as fuel, paper money instead of coins, and papermaking and printing processes. Marco made many notes about life in China.

After almost 20 years in China, the Polos began their journey home to Italy. Kublai Khan gave them many gifts of ivory, silk, jewels, and jade.

When they returned to Venice, they found their city at war. Marco Polo was put in prison. He spent his time writing a book about his years in China. The book is called *Description of the World*. It became the most popular book in Europe. Because of the book, many people in Europe learned about life in China.

Use the passage on page 8 to answer the questions.

1. Which of the following best describes Venice during Marco Polo's time?

    A. It was just like the rest of Europe.

    B. It was a unique city with beautiful buildings and water canals.

    C. Very few merchants came to trade in Venice.

    D. Kublai Khan ruled Venice and all of Italy.

2. Which sentence best states the main idea of this passage?

    A. Travel to China took a long time in 1254.

    B. Kublai Khan welcomed the Polos when they arrived.

    C. Marco Polo could speak four languages.

    D. Marco Polo became famous for writing about his travels in China.

3. Which of the following is not true? When Marco Polo returned to Venice,

    _____.

    A. he became a rich merchant

    B. the city was at war

    C. he was put in prison

    D. he wrote a book

4. Using the details in the passage, fill in the blanks to summarize Marco Polo's trip to China.

    Marco Polo traveled with his _____ and _____

    when he was _____ years old. It took _____ years to get to China. They were

    greeted by _____. On his trips through China, Marco saw

    amazing things such as _____, _____,

    and _____. The Polos stayed in China nearly _____ years.

Read the passage. Then, complete the activities on page 11.

# Deep in the Earth

The earth is covered with rocks of various sizes, colors, and shapes. Rocks may be formed in different ways. Three kinds of rocks are igneous rocks, sedimentary rocks, and metamorphic rocks.

Igneous rocks are formed from extremely high temperatures. Deep inside the earth's core is hot, liquid rock called magma. Magma may be forced through cracks in the earth. As it moves away from the hot core, it cools and forms igneous rock. Sometimes liquid rock is forced to the surface of the earth through volcanoes. When lava from a volcano cools, it forms igneous rock.

Sedimentary rock is formed when loose materials are pressed together over time. These loose materials may be small stones, sand, and decomposed plants and animals. Often the materials accumulate on the bottom of the ocean. The water may dissolve or get pressed out. The loose materials get cemented together as they harden into rock.

Metamorphic rocks are rocks that have been formed by some major change. Pressure and heat can change igneous and sedimentary rocks into metamorphic rocks. Through heat and pressure, the metamorphic rock may change the way it looks or even its mineral makeup.

Each of these rocks can be found on Earth's crust. You can study a rock's properties to help identify whether it is igneous, sedimentary, or metamorphic.

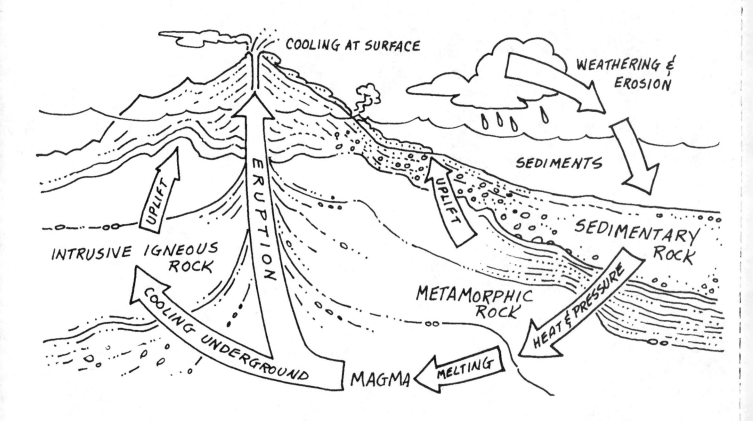

Use the passage on page 10 to complete the activities.

1.  Use one word to name the topic of this passage. _____

2.  The main idea of the passage is _____.

    A.  Fossils are trapped in rocks

    B.  Igneous rocks are formed from magma

    C.  Rocks are formed three ways

3.  Fill in the web. Write the topic sentence in the first oval. Write the three subtopics in the next three ovals. Fill in the rest of the ovals with the supporting details.

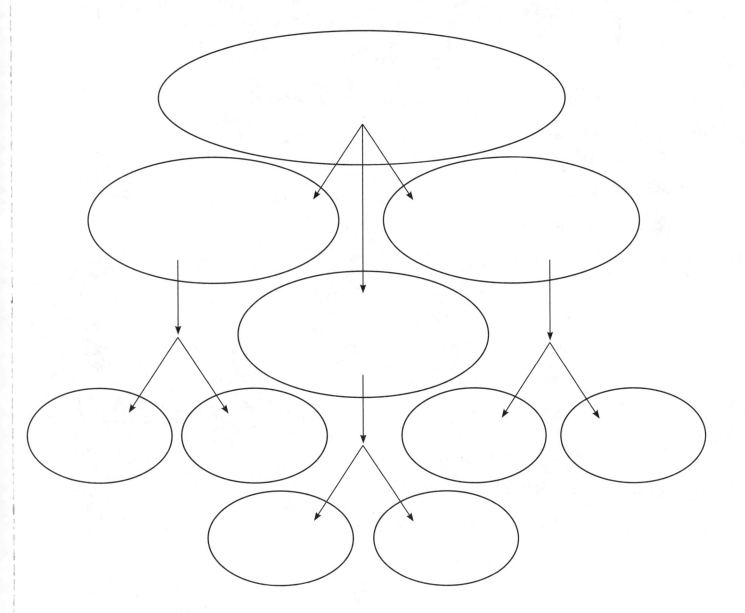

Each paragraph is missing its topic sentence. Read the rest of the paragraph and decide what it is about. Complete the guide below each paragraph to help you write the topic sentence on the last line.

# What's The Point?

1.     It keeps your brain working. It helps you concentrate and not feel tired. Breakfast also gives you the energy to do your best.

Word referent (pronoun): _____

Word it refers to (topic): _____

The point of the paragraph is _____

_____

2.     It can make writing a story or a paper much easier. You can add an idea in the middle of a sentence without rewriting the whole sentence. The computer can also check the spelling for you.

Word referent (pronoun): _____

Word it refers to (topic): _____

The point of the paragraph is _____

_____

3.     They eat grass. They also eat other small plants. In the winter, if green plants are hard to find, deer also eat bark from trees.

Word referent (pronoun): _____

Word it refers to (topic): _____

The point of the paragraph is _____

_____

Read each paragraph. Then, answer the questions.

# Sharp Pencils and Sharp Minds

1.      You need a sharp pencil in order to do quality work. What should you do if your pencil tip breaks while someone is giving instructions? It can be distracting to sharpen your pencil during instruction time. It is important to know when to sharpen your pencil so that learning continues for everyone in the class. Some good times to sharpen a pencil are before or after school and at recess. Another possible time is when people are working, not listening to directions. When students are trying to listen to another student, the teacher, or a video presentation, the pencil sharpener can be distracting or loud enough to make hearing difficult. Keep an extra sharp pencil in your desk so you have a pencil at a time when you may not be able to get to the sharpener.

Topic: _____

Main idea of the paragraph:_____

Two supporting details: _____

_____

_____

2.      Most nine- and ten-year-olds need from nine to 12 hours of sleep each night. Getting enough rest can improve your attitude. It helps your brain stay in the thinking mode rather than falling into the emotional mode. It helps you stay focused on learning and allows you to think clearly. Most rested people get along better with others than their sleepy friends do. They have more energy not only for learning but also for playing.

Topic: _____

Main idea of the paragraph:_____

Two supporting details: _____

_____

_____

Name_____

Read the letter. Then, answer the questions.

# A Night in Texas

Dear Hailey,

   We are in Austin, Texas. You would never believe what I saw tonight. We were in a restaurant by the Congress Avenue Bridge. As the sun was going down, I saw a cloud moving around by the bridge. Do you know what the cloud was? It was a cloud of bats!! The bats live under the bridge. It is dark there during the day because the sun does not shine under the bridge. Also, the sun makes it nice and warm, kind of like my electric blanket at home.

   Well, when the sun started to go down, all of those bats woke up. They were hungry. The waitress said there were over a million of the Mexican free-tailed bats living under the Congress Avenue Bridge. I wanted to know if they attacked the cars or the people walking on the bridge. She laughed and said that bats are gentle animals that may look scary, but they do not attack people or cars.

   Another waitress said the bats were really good because they eat over 10,000 pounds of insects EVERY NIGHT! Gag! Can you imagine eating that many bugs? I weigh about 60 pounds so that's like eating enough insects to make about 170 of me. Boy, maybe we need some of those bats by our house. I sure hated all of those mosquitoes that were trying to eat us last week.

   Well, I've got to go. Don't get too "batty" without me!

                                   Sincerely,
                                   Michaela

1.  Where was Michaela when she wrote the letter? _____

2.  What is the topic of her letter? (one word) _____

3.  Write three details Michaela wrote about her topic. _____

    _____

    _____

4.  Michaela compared several things to other things. Write one comparison here.

    _____ to _____

5.  Write one fact you learned about bats. _____

    _____

    _____

Read the letter. Then, answer the questions.

# Bees

Dear Isabel,

Do you remember the bees we saw last week? We were scared of them. They came by our fresh peach sundaes, so we shooed them away.

I just learned something about bees in school today. Did you know that without bees we would not have all of the fruits, vegetables, and other plants that we have today? Bees help pollinate plants. This is important because if the plants are not pollinated, seeds are not made. If seeds are not made, new plants will not grow. I'd sure hate to give up juicy peaches, sweet cherries, and messy watermelon!

I learned that bees are in trouble. There is a tiny mite, a member of the spider family, that kills baby bees. Other bees are killed by pesticides, or chemicals used to kill bad insects. There used to be enough bees to pollinate farmers' crops. Now some farmers have to pay a beekeeper to bring thousands of bees to the field to pollinate the plants.

I think I am going to be more respectful next time I see a bee. I know they are kind of scary, but they are also very good for our farmers.

Sincerely,
Jayla

1.  What is the author's purpose? _____

2.  What is the main idea of paragraph two?_____

    _____

    Write two supporting details.

    _____

    _____

3.  What is the main idea of paragraph three? _____

    _____

    Write two supporting details.

    _____

    _____

Read the passage. Then, answer the questions.

# Dynamite

Dynamite is one of the most powerful explosives in the world. It is often used to blast away earth. This is needed for building dams, making foundations for large buildings, and for mining. Dynamite is made from a chemical named nitroglycerin. The word **dynamite** comes from a Greek word meaning power.

Dynamite was first produced in 1867 by Alfred Nobel. Nobel was a Swedish chemist who later became famous for using his fortune to establish the Nobel Prizes. His first dynamite was dangerous to use because it exploded so easily. He later developed a way of mixing nitroglycerin with a chalk-like soil. He placed this mixture into hollow tubes, or sticks. This stick dynamite was safer because it would not explode until a blasting cap was added. Nobel later invented a special dynamite, called blasting gelatin, that would explode under water.

1.  Dynamite was made safer by
    _____.

    A. using it only for mining and foundations

    B. using nitroglycerin

    C. producing it in 1867

    D. mixing it with chalk-like soil and putting it in hollow tubes

2.  Which of the following is not true of Alfred Nobel?

    A. He used his fortune to establish the Nobel Prizes.

    B. He was a Swedish chemist.

    C. He won the first Nobel Prize.

    D. He mixed nitroglycerin with a chalk-like soil.

3.  Dynamite that can explode under water is called _____.

    A. nitroglycerin

    B. blasting caps

    C. hollow tubes

    D. blasting gelatin

4.  The word dynamite comes from the Greek word for _____.

    A. famous

    B. explosion

    C. power

    D. dangerous

Name_____

Read the passage. Then, answer the questions.

# A Mexican Fiesta

A common sight at parties (or fiestas) in Mexico is the piñata, a hanging decoration filled with candies, fruits, and small gifts. You can make your own piñata by following the directions below.

1. Inflate a balloon.
2. Dip strips of newspaper into paste (made of flour and water), and cover the balloon. Let it dry.
3. To make animal features or other shapes, use twisted rolls of newspaper and cover them with the paste strips. Be sure to leave a small opening to use later for filling the piñata with prizes.
4. Allow the piñata to dry.
5. Decorate the piñata with paint or small pieces of colored tissue paper that can be glued in different designs.
6. Pop the balloon(s) inside the piñata. Fill the piñata with candies, fruits, and prizes. Use heavy-duty tape or newspaper strips to seal the filling hole.
7. Hang your piñata using string or wire.
8. Blindfold a child, give him a small stick, and lead him near the piñata so he can hit it. Have fun!

1. Which of the following has the steps for making a piñata in the correct order?

   A. allow it to dry, fill with prizes, hang it up

   B. dip strips into newspaper, fill with prizes, inflate balloon

   C. cover the balloon, decorate, allow it to dry

   D. allow it to dry, decorate, inflate balloon

2. True or false? You should be sure not to pop the balloon inside the piñata after it dries.

   _____

3. Maggie is ready to fill a piñata with prizes, but there is no hole to pour them inside. Which step did the person who made the piñata skip?

   _____

Read the passage. Then, answer the questions.

# Northern Lights

You may see them in the north in the nighttime sky. They begin with a slight shimmer in the sky. Within minutes, thin poles of light are rippling across the sky. The lights are greenish or white in the center and slightly violet or red at the edges. They flow like a blanket being shaken out at the beach. They are known as the northern lights, or **aurora borealis**. They will take your breath away for 10 to 20 minutes, then fade away.

The aurora borealis starts on our nearest star, the sun. On the sun, extremely hot gas particles are very excited. They create a state of matter called plasma. This plasma escapes the sun's **corona**, or atmosphere. These particles, called a solar wind, spray out like water from a hose that someone swings in a circle over his head. The solar wind travels through space. If it is aimed at earth, it is attracted to the earth's magnetic field surrounding the north and south poles.

When this solar wind hits the earth's atmosphere, the particles strike atoms. These atoms release a burst of color. The storm of particles hitting the atmosphere is called an aurora substorm. When the plasma particles stop striking, the brilliant light show, called the aurora borealis, stops.

1.  What is another name for the northern lights? _____

2.  How long do the northern lights usually last?_____

3.  Where do the northern lights start? _____

4.  What is a **corona**?_____

5.  What does the solar wind spray out from the sun like? _____

    _____

6.  What is an aurora substorm? _____

7.  What causes the aurora borealis to end? _____

    _____

    _____

Read the passage. Then, complete the activity.

# Great Lakes

Many states border the five Great Lakes in the United States. One state is Michigan. Michigan touches four of the Great Lakes: Lake Michigan, Lake Superior, Lake Huron, and Lake Erie. The Mackinaw Bridge joins the narrow passage where Lake Michigan and Lake Huron meet. Michigan beaches are full during the summer of swimmers and boaters. Michigan supports many state parks that border the Great Lakes.

Wisconsin is a state that touches two Great Lakes. It is on the west side of Lake Michigan and to the south of Lake Superior. Many people launch boats from this state. People catch freshwater fish in all seasons. Tourists visit and enjoy the water of Wisconsin in different ways.

Illinois borders the southern part of Lake Michigan. Chicago is a large city right on the lake. Navy Pier is one Chicago tourist attraction on the lake. Visitors and people from Illinois enjoy the lake for swimming, boating, and viewing.

1.   Underline the topic sentence above and write it in the large oval. Find the three main supporting details. Write them in the next set of ovals. Each supporting detail has minor supporting details. Write one for each in the last set of ovals.

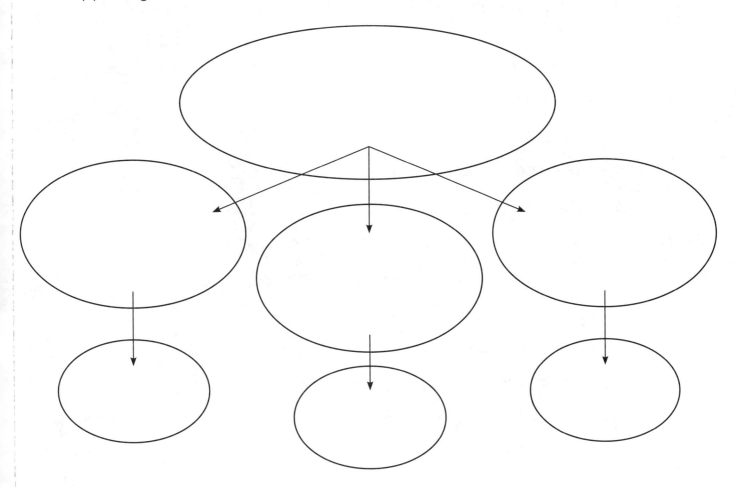

Read the recipe. Then, complete the activity.

# Pizza Recipe

**Ingredients**:
soft tortillas
tomato sauce
shredded mozzarella cheese
your favorite pizza toppings:
    pepperoni, mushrooms,
    pineapple, sausage, olives, etc.

**Directions**:
1. Gather the ingredients, a cookie sheet, and a spoon.
2. Put the tortillas on the cookie sheet.
3. Spoon tomato sauce onto each tortilla. Spread it around to lightly cover the tortilla.
4. Sprinkle each tortilla with mozzarella cheese.
5. Add other toppings that you like.
6. Bake at 350°F (149°C) for about 10 minutes or until cheese is melted.
7. Take out of oven and let cool for 3 to 5 minutes.
8. Remove from cookie sheet and serve.

Use the recipe to answer the questions. Highlight where you found the answers.

1. List three possible toppings for your pizza.

    _____    _____    _____

2. If you like ground beef, could you use it as a topping? _____

    What words tell you this?_____

3. Can hard-shelled tacos be used with this recipe?    Yes    No

4. At what temperature should you bake your pizza? _____

    For how long? _____

5. What ingredient goes on the tortilla first?_____

6. Which goes on first—the toppings or cheese? _____

7. If you could choose any three toppings to go on your pizza, what would they be?

    _____    _____    _____

Read the passage. Then, complete the activity.

# Marshmallows

The stars were bright in the October sky. The full moon cast shadows over the backyard.

The fire burned brightly in the fire pit. The flames glowed orange, then yellow, then red. The logs cracked and popped. Sparks drifted up, floated off, and went out. At the edge of the fire pit were glowing embers. Their colors shifted from black to orange to white.

It was time for roasting marshmallows. Each child found a perfect roasting stick. They speared white marshmallows onto the ends of their sticks.

The two boys and three girls ranged in ages from four to 12. Their parents watched from the four chairs scattered around the fire.

As each marshmallow was roasted a golden brown, it went into a mouth. Then, new marshmallows were popped onto the ends of the sticks and the roasting began again.

1. Draw a picture of the story. Each time you draw a detail, highlight it in the story. Include as many details as you can.

Read the passage. Then, answer the questions on page 23.

# The Summerhouse

Ethan and his family drove around the lake. The road cut through the forest. Ethan could just see the ice blue water through the maples, oaks, and pines. He couldn't wait to go for a swim. Squirrels and other quick animals darted through the trees as the car approached them. Birds called back and forth announcing their arrival at the summerhouse.

The sun was directly overhead when they pulled into the driveway. Ethan could see that the yard needed mowing. It was hard to find grass in all the weeds. He hoped his parents wouldn't mow right away. He could see interesting insects and butterflies flying from wildflower to wildflower. Ethan had brought his bug jar and butterfly net. It looked like he would have lots of insects to add to his collection.

In the middle of the sunny clearing stood the house Ethan's family had rented for the summer. The blue house was two stories tall. Right in the middle of the bottom floor was a wide, bright red door. Upstairs, there were two large, rectangular windows located on each side of the downstairs door. The two windows looked like big, dark eyes. Ethan hoped he could have the room on the left. The branch of an old oak tree reached right under the window. Ethan thought of using it as a way out of his room.

The paint on the house, which had once been blue, was peeling off and looked gray. The roof was jet black, soaking up the heat from the sun. There must have been windows on the first floor, but you couldn't see them hidden behind the overgrown bushes and the large screened porch. Many holes were rusted through the screen, and it was covered with vines that grew as tall as the second floor. Ethan thought the porch would be a great place to make a fort.

Ethan's parents groaned. Ethan stared wide-eyed at the house.

This place was going be quite a summer experience.

Use the passage on page 22 to answer the questions.

Ethan and his parents do not seem to agree about the summerhouse. Ethan thinks it will be a wonderful place. His parents groan. Write about their different viewpoints.

1.  How do they view the yard?

    Ethan's parents see _____ and it makes them think of

    _____

    Ethan sees _____ and it make him think of

    _____

2.  How do they view the house?

    Ethan's parents see _____ and makes them think of

    _____

    Ethan sees _____ and it make him think of

    _____

    Ethan's parents see _____ and makes them think of

    _____

    Ethan sees _____ and it make him think of

    _____

3.  Draw a picture of the summerhouse. Each time you use a detail from the text, highlight it with yellow. Include as many details as you can.

Read the passage. Then, complete the activities on page 25.

# US Paper Money

The United States has its own forms of money, different from all other countries. Money in the United States has changed over time and continues to change to meet the needs of the users.

In the United States, paper money was first issued in 1775. That year, the Continental Congress authorized the **issue**, or giving out, of paper money to finance the Revolutionary War. This "continental currency" soon came to be worth very little and fell out of use. In 1785, the US government decided that the official money system would be based on the dollar. In the 1860s, the United States government issued paper money that looks much like the money we use today. The backs of these bills were printed with green ink. The green ink gave the bills the nickname "greenbacks."

In 1865, the Secret Service was established to control **counterfeits**, or fake money. At that time, about one-third of the money in circulation was counterfeit.

Paper bills feature important people from US history. For example, the one-dollar bill shows a picture of George Washington; the two-dollar bill shows a picture of Thomas Jefferson; and the five-dollar bill shows a picture of Abraham Lincoln. These three men also appear on coins.

Paper money was not always the size it is today. At one time, the bills were larger. In 1929, the bills were all made the same size, which is the size they are today.

In the 1990s, new security features were added to several bills to prevent counterfeiting. Some of these features include color-shifting ink, microprinting, and a security thread. The first bill to be changed was the 100-dollar bill in 1991.

By 1999, only the 1-, 2-, 5-, 10-, 20-, 50-, and 100-dollar bills were still being produced, although bills of higher denominations were still in use. As new bills are made, the old are not immediately taken out of circulation. Paper bills are in constant use and will continue to be updated as the needs of US consumers change.

Name_____

Use the passage on page 24 to complete the time line. Then, answer the questions.

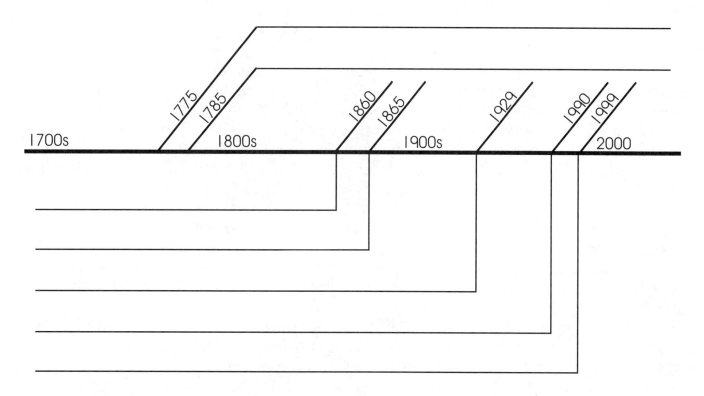

1. What does **counterfeit** mean?_____

2. In what year was the US Secret Service established?_____

   Why? _____

3. What does **issue** mean?_____

4. What gave paper money the nickname "greenbacks"? _____

   _____

5. Which three famous people appear on both bills and coins?_____

   _____

6. What year were all bills changed to one size? _____

7. Why were security features added to paper money in the 1990s? _____

   _____

   _____

Read the passage. Then, answer the questions on page 27.

# Red Tide

The Gulf of Mexico is a body of saltwater that lies between Florida and Central America. It is a place where many people like to go on vacation. The weather is almost always warm. People like to go swimming and play in the sun. And many interesting plants and animals live in the water, such as dolphins, sharks, horseshoe crabs, and sponges. But, once in a while a "red tide" occurs and spoils the fun.

When a red tide occurs, the water turns red. The water may stay red for a couple hours or several months. When the water is red, everyone stays out of it because a red tide can make people sick. A red tide is caused by an organism called a dinoflagellate (di nuh FLAJ uh late) that **multiplies** when the nutrients, sunlight, and water are just right.

People do not like red tides because they know that they might irritate their eyes, nose, and throats. Some people find that their lips and tongues tingle. People with asthma may find it hard to breathe.

Red tides can be poisonous to fish and other **marine**, or saltwater, animals. When the sea animals eat the organisms in a red tide, they are poisoned and die. Other animals die because the organisms use up all of the oxygen in the water, and the sea animals cannot breathe. Many fish wash up on shore during a red tide. The dead fish smell terrible.

Some shellfish eat the red tide and do not die. But the poisons can stay in the bodies of shellfish. When there is a red tide, it is unsafe for people and other animals to eat things like oysters and clams.

Most people do not spend as much time on the beach during red tides. This is because of the heath risks and the smell of rotting marine bodies. However, people who like to look for shells find that a red tide is a good time to collect them. The poisons kill the animals inside the seashells and the shells wash up on the beaches.

Some scientists in western Florida are studying red tides. They hope to be able to learn more about them. Learning more will help scientists understand why they happen. Then, they will be able to warn the people on the coast when the water is not safe.

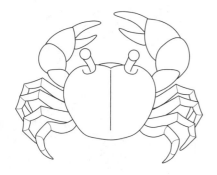  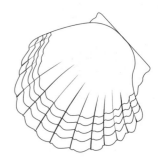

Use the passage on page 26 to answer the questions.

1. Why are scientists studying the red tides? _____

_____

2. What does **marine** mean? _____

3. Name two conditions that seem to cause the red tide to multiply. _____

_____

_____

4. Name three ways a red tide can affect people.

_____

_____

_____

5. What does **multiply** mean? _____

6. What organism causes the red tide? _____

7. What are some nice things about the Gulf of Mexico? _____

_____

_____

8. Why would a person want to stay at the beach during a red tide?

_____

_____

9. What should a person with asthma do when there is a red tide?

_____

_____

Read the advertisement. Then, answer the questions on page 29.

# Book Offer

# GET SIX GREAT BOOKS FOR UNDER A BUCK!

99¢    99¢

## Choose your favorite six books from our huge catalog of great titles.

Write the four-digit code for each book in the spaces on the form below. You will be billed 99¢ for each book, plus tax and shipping and handling.

Here is the deal: Buy six titles today at this incredible price. Then, you only have to purchase six additional books at regular club prices. You have one year to make your purchases.*

Enter your selection numbers here:

_ _ _ _ , _ _ _ _ , _ _ _ _

_ _ _ _ , _ _ _ _ , _ _ _ _

**SPECIAL OFFER!**

Order a seventh book today at only $3.99 and you only have 5 more to go!

_ _ _ _

Name _____

Address _____

City, State, Zip _____

_____ bill me _____ payment enclosed

Credit card number _____

*We reserve the right to substitute titles if the one ordered is out of stock.

Use the advertisement on page 28 to answer the questions.

1. What product is this advertisement trying to sell you?

   A. movies        B. tapes        C. books        D. stocks

2. What is the greatest number of books you can purchase with this form? _____

3. After you buy the first six books, how many books do you need to buy? _____

4. How long do you have to buy them?_____

5. 99¢ is the price for _____.        A. all six books        B. each of the six books

6. Decide whether each statement is true or false. Write **T** for true and **F** for false. Then, go back to the advertisement and highlight where you found the answer.

   _____ You are guaranteed the titles you select.

   _____ You can order one more book for $3.99.

   _____ You can send the payment or have the company bill you.

Write **given** or **not given** to describe whether the advertisement gave you this information. Highlight where you found the answer.

7. How much is shipping and handling?_____

8. What is the average price of a book at "regular club prices"?_____

9. What is the telephone number to call for more information? _____

10. Write two or three sentences telling what you think about this offer. Do you think it is a good deal? Explain your answer.

    _____

    _____

    _____

    _____

    _____

Name_____

Read the passage. Then, complete the activity.

# Which Resource?

Information can be found in many places. Knowing where to look for information can make locating it much faster.

One place to look for factual information is in an **encyclopedia**. An encyclopedia usually has many volumes. Each volume lists topics in alphabetical order.

Another source for information is an **atlas**. An atlas is full of maps. If you're looking for words instead of places, a **thesaurus** is a great tool for finding words that mean about the same thing. A **dictionary** is a good resource to check for spelling, meanings, pronunciations, or for learning how to say a word.

An **index** or **glossary** may be found in the back of some books. An index lists topics in alphabetical order and gives the page numbers where you can find that information. A glossary is like a dictionary of words used within that book.

Read each sentence. Choose the best resource from the passage to find the information.

1. _____ Find the page in the book that tells about limpets.

2. _____ Locate a map of South America.

3. _____ A word in the textbook is in bold print. What is its definition?

4. _____ How do you say "pyrargyrite"?

5. _____ Find five words that mean the same thing as "happy."

6. _____ What are the names and spellings of the world's oceans?

7. _____ Find five facts about kites.

8. _____ You are looking for another word for "great" for your newspaper article.

9. _____ You are working on equivalent fractions and want to know which pages in your math book cover this topic.

Name_____

Read the passage. Then, answer the questions.

# Glue

**Glue** is an adhesive. It is used to stick things together. There are three basic kinds of glue: hide glue, bone glue, and fish glue. Glues are made of gelatin, which comes from boiling animal parts and bones.

Long ago, people used other materials as glue. Ancient people used sticky juices from plants and insects. This was mixed with vegetable coloring and used as paint on rocks and caves. Egyptians learned to boil animal hides and bones to make glue. This was much like the glue that is used today.

Today, there are many special kinds of glue. Epoxy glue is made to stick in high temperatures, even if it becomes wet. "Super" glue is the strongest of glues. It can stick even with two tons of pressure against it.

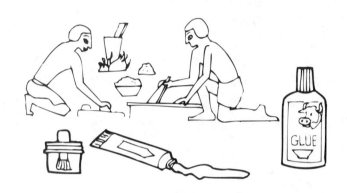

1.  What are the three basic kinds of glue?

    _____ glue

    _____ glue

    _____ glue

2.  Which of the following phrases gives the best definition for glue?

    A. useful for repairs or art activities

    B.  an adhesive used to stick things together

    C.  something that sticks in high temperatures

    D.  mixture of vegetable coloring and bones

3.  Summarize the passage in your own words.

    _____

    _____

    _____

    _____

    _____

    _____

    _____

    _____

    _____

Read the passage. Then, answer the questions.

# Traveling Seeds

Everyone knows that flowering plants cannot fly, run, or walk. But, through their seeds, they can move from place to place. That is why you see new plants growing each year where there were none before.

Flowering plants grow in many different colors and sizes, but they all have seeds. The part of the plant that holds the seeds is called the fruit. Some seeds travel in their fruit. Others fall out and travel to a place where they can grow. But, how do they get to this new place?

Some seeds stick to people's clothes or animals' fur and are carried from place to place. The seeds drop off and form new plants where they fall. Other seeds may be scattered by wind and rain.

However it happens, seeds certainly move.

1. Number the sentences below to summarize correctly one way that seeds could move from place to place.

    _____ Seeds stick to your shirt.

    _____ Seeds form new plants where they fall.

    _____ Seeds fall off of your shirt.

    _____ You walk in a garden.

2. From the passage, you can conclude that seeds ( do,  do not ) move around.

3. Which of the following is not a way that seeds can travel to a new place?

    A.  on your shirt

    B.  in the wind

    C.  on a walking plant

    D.  on a dog

4. From the details in the passage, write a sentence to explain why you see new plants growing in places there were none the year before.

    _____

    _____

    _____

Students in Mia's class were assigned to interview other students about something they were good at. Here is Mia's interview with Daniel.

# Messy Desk

| | |
|---|---|
| Mia: | I noticed that you have a clean desk. What do you do to keep your desk clean? |
| Daniel: | I first decide what has to go into my desk. Then, I find a place for everything and try to keep it in its place. |
| Mia: | How do you find time to do this? |
| Daniel: | On Tuesdays, I take a few minutes to make sure my desk is clean. |
| Mia: | So, you choose a day to work on your desk? |
| Daniel: | Yes. |
| Mia: | Then you only clean your desk on Tuesday? |
| Daniel: | No, whenever I take something out, I try to do it without making a mess. And, when I put something back, I try to put it in its place. |
| Mia: | Does this really work? |
| Daniel: | Most of the time. When it gets a little messy, I know it will get straightened out on Tuesday. |
| Mia: | Thank you for your time, Daniel. |

List four things that help Daniel keep his desk clean. Highlight key words or phrases where you found the information.

1. _____

2. _____

3. _____

4. _____

5. Write an **X** in front of the sentence that would make the best topic sentence for Mia's summary.

_____ Tuesday is a good day to clean desks.

_____ Keeping your desk clean takes planning and time.

_____ Put things back in their place when you are finished with them.

Read each biography. Then, complete the chart on page 35.

# Native American Biographies

### Wilma Mankiller

Wilma Mankiller was born in 1945. She is a Cherokee from Oklahoma. Wilma lived in San Francisco for a long time before returning to Oklahoma. In San Francisco, she learned many skills that could help her as a chief. She became Principal Chief of the Cherokee Nation in 1985. She worked hard for improved health care, civil rights, and many other important causes. Wilma believed in an old Cherokee saying about being of good mind. She called this "positive thinking."

### Crazy Horse

Crazy Horse was known as a fierce warrior of the Lakota tribe who never gave up. Born in 1849, Crazy Horse worked hard to keep the Native American way of life from disappearing. He did not want to lose the customs of his tribe. Most people say that Crazy Horse did not allow pictures to be taken of him, as this was against his beliefs. His image, though, is etched in stone on the Crazy Horse Memorial in South Dakota.

Wilma Mankiller

Crazy Horse

Chief Joseph

Red Cloud

## Native American Biographies (cont.)

### Chief Joseph

Born in 1840, Chief Joseph was given a Native American name that meant *Thunder Rolling Down the Mountain*. Chief Joseph became chief of the Nez Percé tribe. There were many attempts to force Chief Joseph's group onto a small Idaho reservation. At first, Chief Joseph refused to go. Then, he recognized that the military would force him and his people onto the reservation anyway. Chief Joseph wanted peace for his people, so he surrendered to the military.

### Red Cloud

Many believe that Red Cloud was one of the most important Lakota leaders of the nineteenth century. Born in 1822, Red Cloud became a great leader and helped to hold and gain land for the Lakota. Red Cloud's work and the plans to help his people were quite successful. As a result, the United States entered into a treaty that forced the United States to abandon all of its forts in one area. The treaty also promised that the Lakota could keep a great amount of their land.

1. Use the information in the biographies to complete the chart.

| Name | Date Born | Tribe | Accomplishment |
|------|-----------|-------|----------------|
|      |           |       |                |
|      |           |       |                |
|      |           |       |                |
|      |           |       |                |

Before reading the passage on page 37, read each pair of statements and write **C** in front of the statement you believe is correct. After reading the article, go over your choices. Write **X** in front of the correct answer. Write the paragraph number where the correct answer is found.

1. _____ A carapace is a shell.

   _____ A carapace is a sudden drop off.

   paragraph _____

2. _____ Horseshoes are a type of crab.

   _____ Horseshoes are related to spiders.

   paragraph _____

3. _____ A telson is a body part that looks like a tail.

   _____ A telson is a body part used to communicate.

   paragraph _____

4. _____ The horseshoe crab's tail is used as a weapon.

   _____ The horseshoe crab's tail is used to flip itself over.

   paragraph _____

5. _____ The horseshoe crab's blood is red.

   _____ The horseshoe crab's blood is blue.

   paragraph _____

6. _____ Scientists use horseshoe crab blood to stop poisons.

   _____ Scientists use horseshoe crab blood to make poisons.

   paragraph _____

7. _____ Scientists use horseshoe crabs' eyes for research.

   _____ Horseshoe crabs' eyes are used to make a delicious dessert.

   paragraph _____

8. _____ *Limulus polyphemus* is the scientific name for a horseshoe crab.

   _____ *Limulus polyphemus* is the name of a scientist who studies crabs.

   paragraph _____

9. _____ Horseshoe crabs are scavengers who eat ocean garbage.

   _____ Horseshoe crabs eat clams, worms, and invertebrates.

   paragraph _____

Read the passage.

# Horseshoe Crabs

1.  The horseshoe crab lives in oceans around the world.  It is often called a living fossil. The scientific name of this animal is *Limulus polyphemus*. *Limulus polyphemus* has been on earth for about 20 million years, but fossils of its close relatives have been found that are around 500 million years old.

2.  The horseshoe crab is not really a crab. It is related to spiders, scorpions, and ticks. This creature has a domed carapace, or shell, that is shaped a bit like a horseshoe. It has five pairs of legs underneath that end in claws. The mouth is found at the base of these legs. The horseshoe crab eats clams, worms, and invertebrates. It breathes with six pair of special gills called book gills.

3.  The tail of the horseshoe crab is called a telson. It is attached to the shell with a hinge joint. This joint works like our elbow joints. The telson helps the horseshoe crab flip back over after a wave has tipped it upside down.

4.  Most horseshoe crabs spend their lives within four miles of where they hatch. These creatures  begin as two- or three-millimeter eggs. They can grow 24 inches (60 cm), long. As the horseshoe crab grows, it molts, or sheds, its too small shell.

5.  The blood of a horseshoe crab is not red like ours. It has a molecule that turns it a bluish color when exposed to the air. This molecule carries the oxygen through its body.

6.  Scientists use horseshoe crabs in research. Horseshoe crabs have two sets of eyes. One set of eyes, called compound eyes, is made up of many tiny eyes. The other set is simple, like human eyes. Scientists study these eyes to learn how human eyes work.

7.  The horseshoe crab is used for other research. Scientists have found that a fluid in the horseshoe crab can be used to make human blood coagulate, or thicken. Scientists are careful not to harm the horseshoe crabs when they remove the fluid and return them to their homes. Then, scientists use a chemical found in the fluid to stop the effect of some poisons in human blood.

8.  Odd and unique, this creature has lived on this earth for a long time. It is an interesting animal that has proven helpful to scientists and worth looking at to those who run across them at the beach.

Before reading the passage on page 39, read each pair of statements and write **C** in front of the statement you believe is correct. After reading the article, go over your choices. Write **X** in front of the correct answer. Write the paragraph number where the correct answer is found.

1.  _____ Francis Scott Key wrote the words to "The Star-Spangled Banner."

    _____ Francis Scott Key wrote the music for "The Star-Spangled Banner."

    paragraph _____

2.  _____ The song was written during the Revolutionary War.

    _____ The song was written during The War of 1812.

    paragraph _____

3.  _____ Francis Scott Key was a newspaper reporter.

    _____ Francis Scott Key was a lawyer.

    paragraph _____

4.  _____ George Washington was president when the song was written.

    _____ James Madison was president when the song was written.

    paragraph _____

5.  _____ Mr. Key was on a British warship when he wrote the song.

    _____ Mr. Key was in an American fort when he wrote the song.

    paragraph _____

6.  _____ The British were attacking Baltimore.

    _____ The British were attacking Washington, DC.

    paragraph _____

7.  _____ The flag Mr. Key was watching was made by Betsy Ross.

    _____ The flag was made by Mary Pickersgill and her daughter Caroline.

    paragraph _____

8.  _____ The song's original title was "The Defense of Fort McHenry."

    _____ The song's original title was "Oh, How I Love the Flag."

    paragraph _____

Read the passage.

# Star-Spangled Banner

1.  "The Star-Spangled Banner" was written by Francis Scott Key in 1814. The War of 1812 was in its third year.

2.  Dr. Beanes, a friend of Francis Scott Key, was a prisoner on a British ship. Friends contacted Mr. Key, a Washington, DC, lawyer, about the matter. He had to get permission from the president to speak with the British general. Mr. Key went to President Madison and was allowed to visit the British fleet under a flag of truce.

3.  Francis traveled from Washington, DC, to Baltimore. He went aboard a British ship to speak with the general. After talking with Mr. Key, General Ross agreed to let Dr. Beanes go. However, the release had to wait until after the British attacked Baltimore.

4.  Francis Scott Key and Dr. Beanes were moved to another British ship, the *Surprise*. They traveled up the Chesapeake Bay to Fort McHenry. Mr. Key could see the new American flag flying over the fort. The flag was made by Mary Pickersgill and her daughter, Caroline. It was 42 by 30 feet (12.8 by 9.1 m) and had 15 stars and 15 stripes.

5.  The Battle of Baltimore was very noisy and very smoky. It was difficult to see the fort from the ship. It seemed that the British would win the battle and the fort would surrender. As long as the American flag was flying, Mr. Key knew that there was hope. As the sun went down, those on the ship could just make out the American flag. It stormed all night long. In the morning, the storm and the battle were both over. The American flag was still flying.

6.  Francis Scott Key began to write the first words, "Oh, say can you see," on the back of an old letter he had in his pocket. He wrote a bit more, but had to put it away because the British fleet was leaving. He and Mr. Beanes went ashore. Later that night, Mr. Key finished the poem.

7.  The next day, he showed the poem to his brother-in-law, who told him to publish it. His brother-in-law added the title "The Defense of Fort McHenry." Soon, however, everyone was calling it "The Star-Spangled Banner."

8.  "The Star-Spangled Banner" become the US national anthem in 1931. Congress made a decree to give the song its national-anthem status 117 years after its words were composed.

Read the passage. Then, answer the questions.

# Honey

Honey is a bee who lives in a hive in the center of an oak tree. Her hive has more than 70,000 bees. Honey is a worker bee. The worker bees are all female, and they each have a job to do. Some worker bees are nursemaids for the larvae. Other workers are cleaners. Some workers guard the entrance of the hive and some, like Honey, collect nectar from flowers.

Honey follows directions given by another bee to find nectar. Today, a bee dances the directions to a blueberry patch. Honey takes off. She flies along a creek until she gets to a sugar maple. She turns and flies through a group of pines, beside a fallen oak, and over a field of clover. She passes seven large rocks, then goes under a vine and finally reaches the blueberry patch.

The petals of the blueberry blossoms make a landing strip for Honey. They direct her to the nectar in the center. Honey sips the nectar from several blossoms. She stores the nectar in her honey sac. In the honey sack, the nectar mixes with her saliva. Honey retraces her flight back to the hive where she empties the liquid from her honey sac into the wax cells of the hive.

During the six weeks she is alive, Honey will return repeatedly to the blueberry field for more nectar. Before she dies, Honey will have made about one teaspoonful of honey to help feed the hive.

1. Name three jobs worker bees can have. _____

   _____

2. How much honey does a bee make during its lifetime? _____

3. How does a honeybee find a plant? _____

4. Number the following statements to put them in the correct sequence.

   _____ Honey gets directions to the blueberry patch.

   _____ Honey uses the petals of the flower for a landing strip.

   _____ Honey brings nectar back to the hive.

   _____ Honey stores nectar in her honey sac.

   _____ Honey flies along the creek until she gets to the sugar maple.

Read the passage. Then, complete the activity.

# Florida and Michigan

Michigan and Florida are both peninsula states. Each is surrounded by water on all sides but one. The water attracts tourists to both states.

Florida is bordered by saltwater. On the west side is the Gulf of Mexico and on the east side, the Atlantic Ocean. Different ocean creatures can be found in these waters, such as sharks, jellyfish, and dolphins. Guests can find seashells along the shores.

Michigan, on the other hand, is bordered by freshwater lakes. It touches four of the Great Lakes. Many freshwater fish, such as salmon and trout, swim in the lakes. Fishermen catch these and other fish. Guests love the sandy beaches and sand dunes.

Michigan and Florida are found in different parts of the United States. Florida is in the south. It is warm in Florida all year round. This allows farmers to grow crops such as oranges and coconuts. Michigan is found in the north. It has four seasons with great ranges in temperature. It is hot in the summer and cold and snowy in the winter. Autumn is a beautiful time in Michigan. In the autumn, the leaves on the trees change colors and then fall to the ground. Many fruits such as blueberries, apples, cherries, and peaches are grown in Michigan.

1.  Compare the information about Florida and Michigan using the Venn diagram.

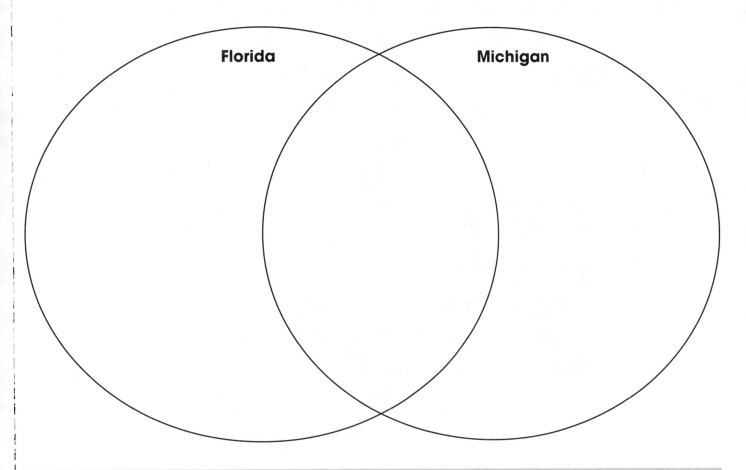

Henry brought home two fliers. Compare the fliers. Then, complete the activities.

# Two Events

**COME TO THE FAMILY FUN CARNIVAL!**
Saturday from 2:00-6:00 pm
All Events are Free!
A brief outdoor program will
begin at 5:00 pm.
Program will include
music,
puppets, and a raffle!
**GAMES    PRIZES    PIZZA    POP**
**HAYRIDES**
**PONY RIDES    FACE PAINTING**
**PETTING ZOO**
We hope you can come!
Sponsored by the Young Child Organization

Every Wednesday this month,
**the County Nature Center**
presents
**"POND LIFE"**
from 7:00 - 8:00 pm.

**BRING BOOTS OR WADERS.**
**NETS AND MAGNIFYING GLASSES**
**ARE PROVIDED.**
**There is no charge for this class.**
Fieldguides and other supplies
will be available for purchase.

1.  Circle the event that is appropriate. You may circle both events.

    Which event takes place outside?          Carnival          Pond Life

    You can attend this event with no money.   Carnival          Pond Life

    At which event will you see live animals?  Carnival          Pond Life

    This event has a raffle.                   Carnival          Pond Life

2.  Which event asks participants to bring something? _____

    They are asked to bring _____ or _____

    Why do you think they are asked to bring it? _____

3.  Henry's father promised to bring him to one event. His dad works weekends.

    Which event will they most likely attend?_____

4.  Name one thing that is common to both events. _____

5.  Read each sentence. Write **T** if it is true or **F** if it is false.

    _____ There will be a petting zoo at the nature center program.

    _____ The carnival has free food.

    _____ A field guide can be purchased at the nature center.

    _____ A school is sponsoring both events.

Read the passage. Then, complete the activity.

# Temperature Rising

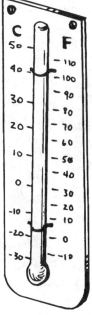

Can you imagine a hot summer day with a temperature of 30 degrees? Or having a fever of 38 degrees that sends you to the doctor? If you're thinking in degrees Fahrenheit, you're probably confused. Another way to measure temperature is in degrees Celsius. The temperature scales on most thermometers show both Fahrenheit and Celsius.

An early version of a thermometer was made in 1593. Gabriel Fahrenheit invented the first mercury thermometer in 1714. The Fahrenheit scale is named after him. On the Fahrenheit scale, water freezes at 32°F, water boils at 212°F, and normal body temperature is 98.6°F.

Anders Celsius was a Swedish astronomer born in 1701. He experimented with a scale based on 100 degrees. On the Celsius scale, water freezes at 0°C, water boils at 100°C, and normal body temperature is 37°C.

1. Fill in the chart below to compare the Fahrenheit and Celsius scales.

| | **Fahrenheit** | **Celsius** |
|---|---|---|
| Invented by | | |
| Water freezes | | |
| Normal body temperature | | |
| Water boils | | |

Read the passage. Then, answer the questions and complete the activity on page 45.

# John Glenn

On October 29, 1998, Senator John Glenn traveled into space as the oldest astronaut ever. He was 77 years old.

This was not the first time Glenn was in space. At 40 years old, Glenn was the first American to circle Earth. During that trip in 1962, he traveled on the *Friendship 7*. He **orbited**, or went around, the earth three times. He was the only person onboard the *Friendship 7* and had only one window to look out. That space ship had no computers onboard. Glenn talked to people on earth while he was in space. They wanted to observe his reaction to the space environment.

In 1998, Glenn went into space on the space shuttle *Discovery*. This time, he was not alone. There were six other astronauts on board the *Discovery* with him. The *Discovery* crew orbited the earth 144 times. They had 10 windows to look out. They also had five computers helping them. This time, scientists wanted to observe the reaction of an older man in the space environment.

Glenn was an American hero in 1962 for orbiting the earth. He became a hero again in 1998 when he traveled as the oldest astronaut to orbit the earth.

1. Why was John Glenn a hero in 1962? _____

_____

2. Why was John Glenn a hero in 1998? _____

_____

3. What does **orbited** mean? _____

_____

4.  In the article on page 44, highlight key facts about the 1962 flight and the 1998 flight. Use the information to fill in the Venn diagram below. Write at least three facts for each year and three facts that the two flights share.

**John Glenn's Space Flights**

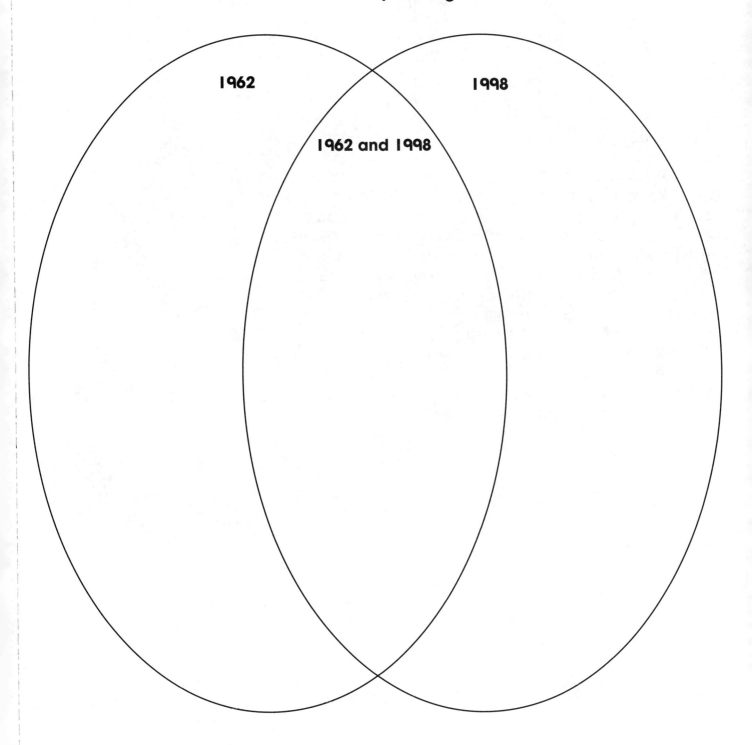

1962

1998

1962 and 1998

Read the passage. Then, complete the Venn diagram on page 47.

# The Underground Railroad

The Underground Railroad had no tracks, no caboose, and no engine. In fact, the Underground Railroad wasn't a railroad at all. It was a group of people who helped slaves escape to freedom. It is believed that the Underground Railroad helped thousands of slaves reach freedom between 1830 and 1860.

The people who led the escape efforts of the Underground Railroad were called "conductors," just like the conductors of a train. The people escaping were called "passengers," just like train passengers. And, the places where the escaping passengers stopped for help were often called "stations," just like the places trains stop at.

Like a train ride, the Underground Railroad moved people along, but in very different ways. Escaping slaves and their conductors often followed routes that had been laid out by others before them. Some escape routes went underground through dirt tunnels, while other routes led across rivers and through rough wilderness and mountain areas. They rarely traveled during the day, finding that it was safer to travel at night.

Conductors and other people who disliked slavery helped escaping slaves find food, drinking water, and places to sleep and hide on their way to freedom. Two of the most famous conductors of the Underground Railroad were Levi Coffin and escaped slave Harriet Tubman.

1. Use the passage on page 46 to complete the Venn diagram.

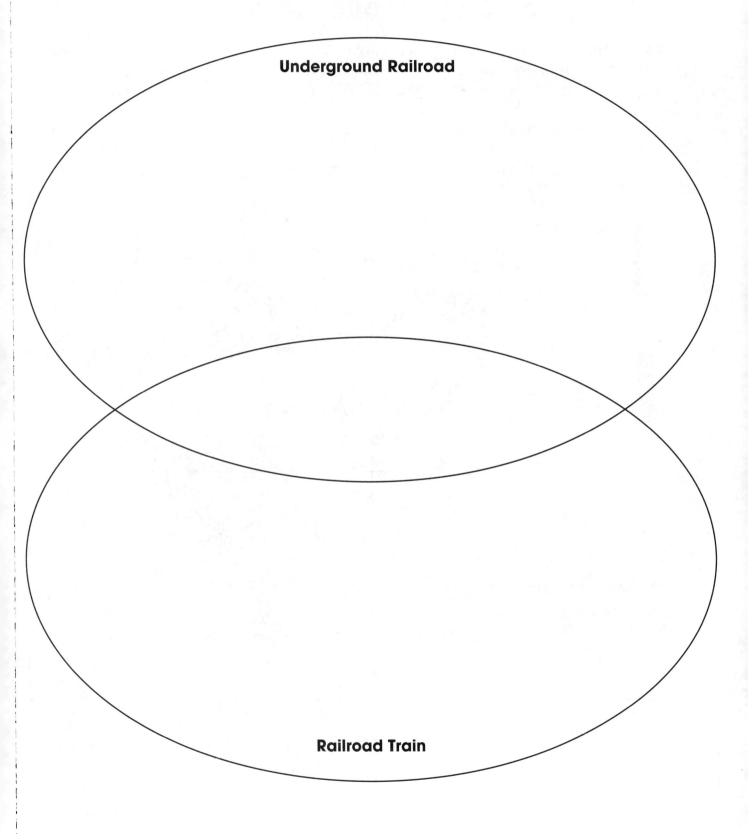

**Underground Railroad**

**Railroad Train**

Read the passage. Then, complete the activity.

# Coin Collecting

Numismatics, or coin collecting, is a very old hobby. It was not popular right away in America. Most Americans were too busy building a country out of a wilderness to think about collecting coins. It was not until about 1840 that Americans began to become serious coin collectors.

Coins are made in factories called mints. From 1792 to 1857, the United States made a cent coin that was as big as our current 50-cent piece. In 1857, the United States stopped making the large-sized cent. When the big coins were hard to get, some people began the hobby of coin collecting.

Coin collecting became popular in the United States in the 1840s. Today, clubs are open to new coin collectors. There are many books and websites about numismatics. You can also visit coin dealers for information and advice.

1.  Use information from the passage to complete the cause and effect chart.

| Cause | Effect |
| --- | --- |
|  | Coin collecting was not popular in the United States before 1840. |
|  | Many people began collecting the large-sized cent. |
|  | Today you can buy coin collecting books and join numismatics clubs. |

Read the passage. Then, complete the activity.

# Dry Ice

Do you know what dry ice is or how it is used? Dry ice is the common name for solid carbon dioxide. Carbon dioxide is a chemical.

When regular ice melts, it changes from a solid piece of ice into a liquid. But dry ice does not melt into a liquid. It changes from a solid piece of ice into a gas. Dry ice can be as cold as -112°F (-80°C). That is much colder than ordinary ice. Although it is safe to eat ordinary ice, dry ice is too dangerous to eat. Because it is extremely cold.

What is dry ice used for? It is used to refrigerate many things that need to be kept cold. Many foods are packed and sent from place to place in dry ice. Because dry ice does not melt into a liquid, it can keep food frozen for several days.

Write **dry ice** or **regular ice** to show the cause of each effect given.

1.  An ice cube leaves a puddle of water on a table. _____

2.  A cheesecake is kept frozen for several days. _____

3.  Ice is eaten safely. _____

4.  A solid melts into a gas. _____

5.  Foods are packed in ice to be shipped. _____

6.  The temperature of a solid piece of ice is -110°F (-19°C). _____

Read the passage. Then, complete the activities on page 51.

# The Storm

The wind howled and the rain beat down. Lightning blazed with a quick light. Thunder crashed. The storm knocked down a towering oak down the street. It knocked out the electricity for the entire street. Wayne sat in front of the dark TV set. He found a flashlight and turned it on.

Wayne shone the flashlight ahead of him as he walked down the hallway. As he entered the kitchen, the flashlight batteries died. The room became inky black. Wayne ran into the wall and stubbed his toe. He hollered and jumped on one foot. He bumped into the table, which upset his marble jar. The jar fell over. The marbles scattered all over the table and floor.

Wayne's dog, Muttsie, jumped up at the noise and ran toward Wayne's voice. Muttsie skidded on the marbles. She flew across the floor into her dog dishes, spilling water and food all over.

The cat, Kitty, was showered with water. She jumped to the safety of the counter. She landed on the edge of a cookie sheet sticking out of the dish rack. The cookie sheet flipped over, taking the contents of the dish rack with it. The pots, plates, and silverware made an awful racket as they hit the floor. One of the pans struck the flour canister. The flour spilled, covering everything in white.

Wayne's mother heard the noise and came running with another flashlight. Amazed, she walked into the kitchen and stopped. "What happened here?" she asked.

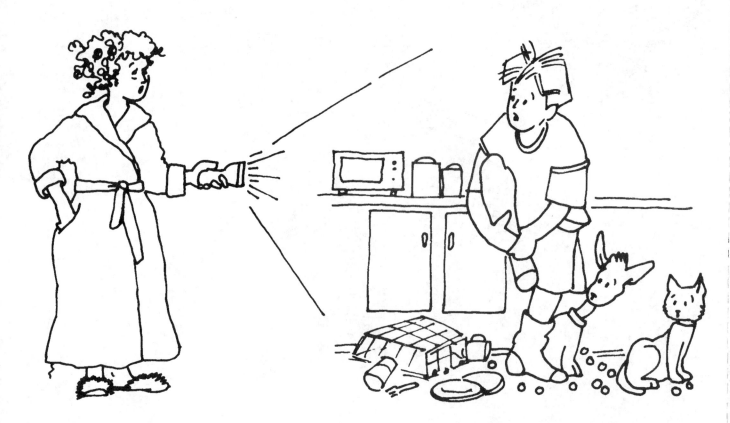

Name_____

Use the passage on page 50 to compete the activities.

1.  Draw a picture showing one cause with its effect.

|  |
|  |
|  |

2.  Fill in the blanks of the cause and effect chart. Remember, an effect can also be a cause for a new effect. The events are not in order.

| Cause | Effect |
|---|---|
| The storm blew down the oak tree. |  |
|  | The TV was dark. |
| Kitty got wet. |  |
|  | Muttsie jumped up. |
| The pots, plates, and silverware fell. |  |
|  | Wayne stubbed his toe on the wall. |
| Wayne bumped into the table. |  |
|  | The cookie sheet tipped over the dish rack. |
|  | Muttsie skidded on the floor. |
| The flour spilled. |  |
|  | Mom came into the room. |

Read the passage. Then, answer the questions.

# Bonnie Blair

Speed skater Bonnie Blair is the only American woman to have won five Olympic gold medals. She is known as one of the best speed skaters in the world.

Born on March 18, 1964, Bonnie was the youngest in a speed-skating family. Her five older brothers and sisters were champion skaters who encouraged her. They put a pair of skates over Bonnie's shoes when she was two years old because there weren't any skates small enough for her tiny feet.

As Bonnie grew, she trained hard six days a week, always pushing to improve her time. Bonnie kept this up until she was the world's best female speed skater. She won her first Olympic gold medal in the 500-meter race in 1988. In 1992, she won both the 500-meter and the 1,000-meter Olympic races in Albertville, France. She repeated her victories in 1994 in Lillehammer, Norway.

Bonnie's Olympic successes made her famous all over the world. Bonnie retired from speed skating in 1995 to focus on other competitions.

Answer the questions in complete sentences.

1. What was the effect of Bonnie being born into a speed-skating family?

_____

_____

2. What caused Bonnie's brothers and sisters to place skates over her shoes?

_____

_____

3. What was the effect of Bonnie's practice and hard work?

_____

_____

Read the passage. Then, answer the questions.

# Clouds

Do you like to watch clouds float by? You may have noticed that there are many different shapes of clouds. Clouds are named for the way they look. Cirrus clouds are thin and high in the sky. Stratus clouds are low and thick. Cumulus clouds are white and puffy.

Do you know how clouds are formed? The air holds water that the warm sun has pulled, or evaporated, from Earth. When this water cools in the air, it forms clouds. When a cloud forms low along the ground, it is called fog.

Clouds hold water until they become full. Warm clouds that are full of water produce rain; cold clouds that are full of water produce snow. When water falls to Earth as either rain or snow, it is called precipitation.

1.  What is the effect of water cooling in the air?

    A.  Evaporation occurs.

    B.  The sun warms Earth.

    C.  Fog forms.

    D.  Clouds form.

2.  Which sentence explains what causes fog?

    A.  A cloud forms low to the ground.

    B.  A cloud is white and puffy.

    C.  A cloud is thin and high in the sky.

    D.  A cloud is full.

3.  One effect of evaporation is _____ .

    A.  rain creates moisture in the soil

    B.  the air holds water

    C.  clouds float through the sky

    D.  the sun pulls clouds higher

4.  Write three short sentences that explain how clouds are formed.

    _____

    _____

    _____

    _____

Read the passage. Then, complete the activity.

# Diamonds

Everyone knows diamonds are the most beautiful stones on Earth. But, did you know that a diamond is the hardest substance found in nature? Diamonds are crystals made of carbon. Scientists believe that diamonds were formed long ago when parts of Earth were under great pressure and heat. Diamonds are so hard that they are used to cut many other hard materials. But, a diamond can only be cut by another diamond or by a synthetic material called borazon.

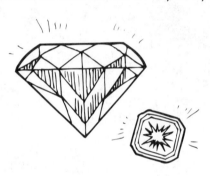

Diamonds are found in just a few places in the world. Miners must dig into the soil and rock to remove the diamonds. Sometimes, tons of earth must be removed and crushed to find just one small diamond. It is worth the effort to find these beautiful jewels.

There have been many famous diamonds in history. The largest, found in 1905, weighed one and one-third pounds (0.6 kg). Even small diamonds are something people enjoy more than any other jewel.

1. Fill in the chart below using information from the passage. Include at least three facts and three opinions about diamonds.

| Facts | Opinion |
|-------|---------|
|       |         |

Read the passage. Then, complete the activities.

# Marie Curie

One of the greatest scientists of all time is Marie Curie. Marie Curie was born in Poland in 1867. She studied at a university in Paris and lived in France for most of her adult life. Along with her husband, Pierre Curie, she studied radioactivity. She was awarded the Nobel Prize in chemistry in 1911 for her work discovering radium and polonium.

The discovery of radium was a turning point in history. Some medical advances based on the research of the Curies are the X-ray and the use of radiation to treat cancer.

The Curies were both generous people. Even though they were poor for most of their lives, they did not patent any of their discoveries so that everyone could benefit from their research. Marie Curie died in 1934. The world should not forget her.

Read each sentence. Write **F** if it is a fact or **O** if it is an opinion.

1. _____ Marie Curie is one of the greatest scientists of all time.

2. _____ Marie Curie was awarded the Nobel Prize in chemistry in 1911.

3. _____ The Curies studied radioactivity.

4. _____ The discovery of radium was the most important turning point in history.

5. _____ The Curies did not patent any of their discoveries.

6. _____ The world should never forget the Curies.

7. Write one fact from the passage. Then, write one opinion from the passage.

_____

_____

_____

_____

Read the passage. Then, answer the questions.

# Sports Report

### "My View in Sports"
by Jack Park

Friday's game against the Wild Ones tallied up another loss for the pathetic Dogs. They were terrible. It was hard to tell if the players were basketball players or golfers. Katz led his sad team against the Wild Ones. Katz made a beautiful shot from half court to bring the Dogs' score to 12 at the end of the exciting first quarter. Shaw scored four perfect three-pointers in the final quarter, but the Wild Ones were too far ahead. The previously winning Dogs should quit turning tail and go on the attack if they have any hope of making the playoffs again this year.

The Mudpies and the Quicksanders played an outstanding game. It was difficult to tell which would find solid ground as the score teeter-tottered back and forth through the whole game. The dependable Gladd put the Quicksanders on top at the last second with a score of 78 to 77. He made an awesome dunk just before the buzzer went off.

Across town, the fabulous Kilometers outdistanced the Miles with a final score of 86–68. The lightning bolt known as Dolby scored half of the Kilometers' 86 points. This 6-foot-8-inch giant should go places. The Miles' two starting forwards, Van Inch and McYard, were also impressive with 22 points each. Both of these blue-ribbon teams have a shot at this year's title.

Locate and highlight at least seven opinion words. Write three facts from each paragraph.

1. The game between the Dogs and the Wild Ones.

   _____

   _____

2. The game between the Mudpies and the Quicksanders.

   _____

   _____

3. The game between the Kilometers and the Miles.

   _____

   _____

Read the passage. Then, answer the questions.

# Stonehenge

Stonehenge is an ancient monument made up of a group of huge stones. It is located in Wiltshire, England. It is not known who put them there or what they really mean. Some scientists believe that they were put there thousands of years ago by people who worshipped the sun.

Over the years, many of the original stones fell or were carried away and used to build other things. But, many stones still stand in place. From these stones and other markings, scientists believe they know how the monument looked when it was first built. Some scientists believe that Stonehenge was built by ancient people to study the sun. These people may have used the monument to predict changes in the seasons—even eclipses of the sun.

Stonehenge is one of the most popular tourist stops in England today.

1. Which of the following is a fact about Stonehenge?

   A. Scientists know what Stonehenge looked like when it was first built.

   B. Stonehenge is located in Wiltshire, England.

   C. Scientists know why Stonehenge was built.

   D. Stonehenge helped people study eclipses of the sun.

2. Which of the following is an opinion about Stonehenge?

   A. Some of the stones were carried away.

   B. Stonehenge is in England.

   C. The stones are in a circle.

   D. Stonehenge is the most popular tourist stop in England.

3. Read each sentence. Write **T** if it is true or **F** if it is false.

   _____ Over the years, many stones fell or were carried away.

   _____ Only five stones remain as a monument.

   _____ Ancient people may have used the monument to study the sun.

   _____ Stonehenge was built hundreds of years ago.

Read each statement. Write **F** if it is a fact or **O** if it is an opinion. If it is an opinion statement, highlight the word or words that helped you to decide.

# Think About It

1. _____ The Pilgrims worked so hard they deserved a feast.

2. _____ Dr. Maulana Karenga is the teacher who founded Kwanzaa.

3. _____ Hexagonal plates and stellar dendrites are different types of snowflakes.

4. _____ "The Star Spangled Banner" is a beautiful song.

5. _____ John Adams was the second president of the United States.

6. _____ Right triangles are easy to make.

7. _____ A square is a type of rectangle.

8. _____ The Gateway Arch is the tallest memorial in the United States.

9. _____ Dr. Seuss wrote and illustrated more than 40 books.

10. _____ E.B. White was a great author.

11. _____ Jesse Owens won four gold medals in the 1936 Olympics.

12. _____ Plants need light and water to grow.

13. _____ African violets are beautiful but hard to keep alive inside.

14. _____ The life cycle of a frog is interesting.

15. _____ Graphs are easy to make and to read.

Read the passage. Then, answer the questions.

# The Milky Way

The Milky Way galaxy is a part of outer space made up of Earth, its solar system, and all the stars you can see at night. There are over 100 billion stars in the Milky Way.

The Milky Way is shaped much like a CD. It has a center that the outer part goes around.

The Milky Way is always spinning slowly through space. It is so large that it would take 200 million years for the galaxy to turn one complete time.

Many stars in the Milky Way are in clusters. Some star clusters contain up to one million stars!

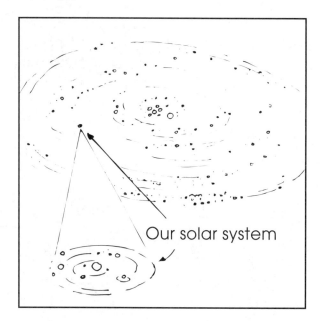
Our solar system

1.  Which of the following correctly lists the objects from smallest to largest?

    A.  Earth, solar system, galaxy

    B.  solar system, star, Earth

    C.  galaxy, solar system, star

    D.  solar system, Earth, galaxy

2.  How are Earth and the solar system related?

    A.  They both are forms of star clusters.

    B.  They are seen at night.

    C.  The solar system is part of Earth's atmosphere.

    D.  Earth is part of the solar system.

3.  Describe the Milky Way galaxy.

    _____

    _____

    _____

    _____

    _____

4.  Which has more stars, a star cluster or the Milky Way?

    _____

5.  Which is larger, a star or a star cluster?

    _____

Read the passage and review the diagram. Then, answer the questions on page 61.

# Symphony Instruments

Emily is going with her father to hear the symphony orchestra. She likes listening to the violins. Her father likes listening to the woodwinds and brass. When she arrives, her father explains that the orchestra musicians must be seated in special places in order to make the music sound just right. The diagram below shows where musicians normally sit in an orchestra.

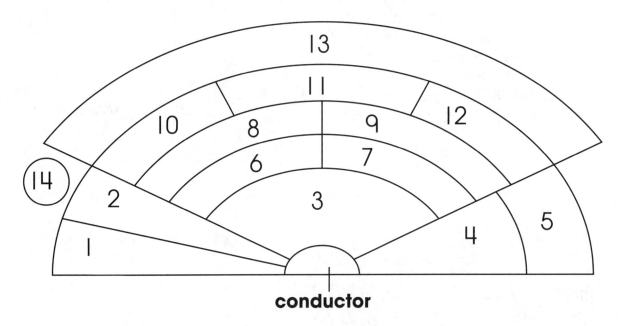

**conductor**

| **Strings** | **Woodwinds** | **Brass** |
|---|---|---|
| 1. First Violins | 6. Flutes | 10. Horns |
| 2. Second Violins | 7. Oboes | 11. Trumpets |
| 3. Violas | 8. Clarinets | 12. Trombones/Tuba |
| 4. Cellos | 9. Bassoons | 13. Percussion/Timpani |
| 5. Double Basses | | 14. Harp |

Name_____

Use the diagram on page 60 to answer the questions.

1. How many types of instruments are in the string section? _____

2. Oboes are in the _____ section.

3. Bassoons are in the _____ section.

4. Number 6 in the diagram stands for _____.

   This instrument is in the _____ section.

5. Who sits farther from the double basses—the trombones or the clarinets?

   _____

6. Who sits closer to the first violins—the horns or the double basses?

   _____

7. Does the conductor stand closer to the violas or the harp?

   _____

8. Is the harp closer to the horns or the tuba?

   _____

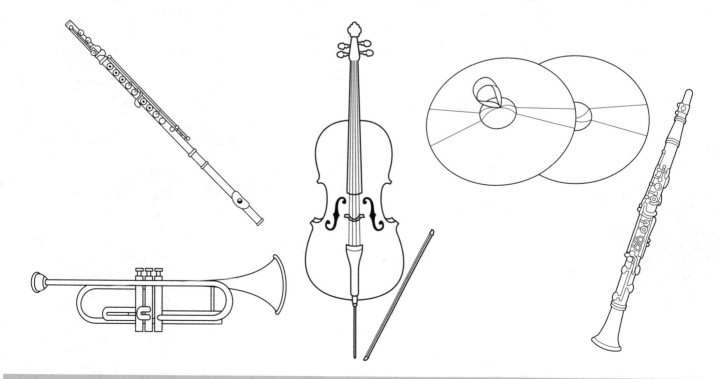

Read the passage. Then, answer the questions.

# A Hurricane

A hurricane is a powerful storm that forms over warm tropical oceans. A hurricane can be several hundred miles wide. Hurricanes are given names beginning with each letter of the alphabet except for Q, U, X, Y, and Z.

A hurricane has two main parts: the eye and the wall cloud. The eye is the center of the storm. In the eye, the weather is calm. The storm around the eye is called the wall cloud. It has strong winds and heavy rain. To be classified as a hurricane, the wind must be at least 74 miles (119 km) an hour. In some hurricanes, the wind can blow over 150 miles (241 km) an hour. A storm with wind less than 74 miles (119 km) an hour can be called a tropical storm.

As the storm moves across the water, it causes giant waves in the ocean. As the storm moves over land, it can cause floods, destroy buildings, and harm people who have not taken shelter.

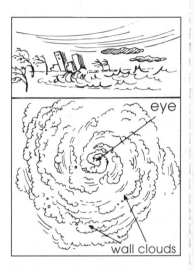
eye
wall clouds

1. Which of the following would not meet the requirements for a storm to be classified a hurricane?

   A. a storm with winds of 74 mph (119 km)

   B. a storm with winds of 70 mph (112 km)

   C. a storm with winds of 150 mph (241 km)

   D. a storm with winds of 87 mph (140 km)

2. A hurricane has which of the following parts?

   A. an eye

   B. a nose

   C. a foot

   D. an arm

3. Fill in the following report by checking all the items that apply to a hurricane. A hurricane _____.

   A. _____ can be several hundred miles wide

   B. _____ can have winds over 150 mph

   C. _____ is a small storm

   D. _____ can cause giant waves in the ocean

   E. _____ is not given a name

4. What is one thing that can happen when a hurricane moves over land?

_____

_____

_____

_____

Read the passage. Then, answer the questions.

# Barbed Wire

Everyone knows what barbed wire is, but do you know why it was such an important invention?

Before barbed wire was invented in 1873, many farmers and ranchers planted shrubs as a fence to keep their cattle from wandering away. They mostly planted osage orange, a thick shrub covered with thorns. This method was often unsuccessful. Some farmers used a plain wire fence, but cattle could break through it and escape.

In 1873, a farmer named Joseph Glidden invented a new kind of wire fence called barbed wire. He fastened pieces of short wire barbs onto the plain wire of a fence. This made it painful for cattle if they tried to push through the fence. Glidden's invention was a huge success. Cattle no longer wandered onto the railroad tracks. This helped the railroad companies build new lines in the western territory. So in many ways, the simple invention of barbed wire helped settle the western frontier.

1. Which of these statements best expresses the author's purpose for this passage?

    A. To convince farmers not to plant osage orange shrubs.

    B. To inform ranchers of the latest techniques for cattle control.

    C. To tell about the life of Joseph Glidden.

    D. To explain why the invention of barbed wire was so important.

2. Which sentence from the passage best helps you understand how the author feels about barbed wire?

    A. This made it painful for cattle if they tried to push through the fence.

    B. Do you know why it was such an important invention?

    C. Cattle no longer wandered onto the railroad tracks.

    D. Many farmers and ranchers planted shrubs.

3. Explain two ways farmers tried to contain their cattle before 1873.

_____

_____

4. How did the invention of the barbed wire fence help settle the western frontier?

_____

_____

Read the passage. Then, answer the questions on page 65.

# Ferdinand Magellan

The early 1500s were an exciting time of exploration and discovery. During this time, a young nobleman named Ferdinand Magellan became excited over the idea of exploring new lands. Magellan told King Charles I of Spain about his plan to look for the Spice Islands. The king agreed to give Magellan ships and supplies.

On September 21, 1519, Magellan and 240 men sailed from Spain in five ships: *Concepcion, San Antonio, Santiago, Trinidad*, and *Victoria*. Magellan sailed across the Atlantic Ocean to South America. He sailed along the coast of South America looking for a place to sail through to the other side of the land. He found a passage near the tip of South America. This passage led from the Atlantic Ocean to another ocean. Today this passage is called the **Strait of Magellan**. Magellan named this other ocean the Pacific Ocean because the waters were so calm.

By the time Magellan reached the Pacific Ocean, he had only three ships left. The *San Antonio* had secretly sailed back to Spain. The *Santiago* had been wrecked in a storm.

Magellan expected to find the Spice Islands soon after entering the Pacific Ocean. But, the three ships sailed west day after day. Many sailors died of hunger or disease. Finally, they reached the Philippine Islands. It was here that Magellan was killed in 1521.

Magellan's ships and crew finally reached the Spice Islands. But, as they sailed home to Spain, the *Trinidad* and the *Concepcion* were wrecked by storms. On September 6, 1522, three years after leaving Spain, the *Victoria* arrived back home. It had sailed around the world.

Although Magellan did not live to complete the voyage, he is known as the first person to sail around the world. It was his voyage that first proved that Earth is round.

Use the passage on page 64 to answer the questions.

1.  In this passage, the author includes mostly _____.

    A.  opinions about Magellan

    B.  facts about Magellan

    C.  made-up stories about sailor life

    D.  scientific information about sailing

2.  The author's goal in writing this passage is most likely _____.

    A.  to talk about shipwrecks

    B.  to tell why Magellan died

    C.  to explain why Earth is round

    D.  to share facts about Magellan's life and explorations

3.  Which of the following book titles would you guess was something written by the same author as this selection?

    A.  *Earth Science for Sailors*

    B.  *Spice Supply Cabinets*

    C.  *Famous Explorers of the 1500s*

    D.  *Fishing in the Pacific Ocean*

4.  Can you guess the definition of the word **strait** from what the author writes in the second paragraph?

    A.  a narrow passage connecting two oceans

    B.  a small river

    C.  an ocean breeze

    D.  a rushing current

Read the passage. Then, answer the questions on page 67.

# Commercials

Television commercials catch our attention. They can be entertaining and make you think. They can make you laugh or cry. They can make you happy, excited, or even angry. Some are even better than the television programs they interrupt. Commercials may stay in our minds for days, months, or even years.

Companies pay large amounts of money to put commercials on television. Why do they pay? They want to sell us something. The purpose of a commercial is to make us believe that we need whatever it is selling. It can be a toy, a pizza, toothpaste, or even a vacation trip. Commercial makers are very good at convincing you.

Don't let the commercial convince you of something that is not true, though! After you watch a commercial, you should think about it. Decide what the commercial is trying to sell you. Decide whether this is something you want. Decide whether you really need it. Ask yourself if it is worth the money. Finally, decide whether you will be as happy with it when you get it home as the commercial makes you think. You must be careful not to let the commercial tell you what you want and need.

The next time you feel a commercial triggering your "need button," think about its purpose. If you cannot say no to commercials, perhaps the "off button" is the one you should push!

Use the passage on page 66 to answer the questions.

1.  What is the author's purpose of this passage? _____

    _____

    Highlight details that helped you decide this.

2.  What are some good things about commercials?_____

    _____

3.  What might be bad about commercials?_____

    _____

4.  What is a "need button"? _____

5.  What is an "off button"? _____

6.  Think of something you bought after seeing a commercial. What was it?

    _____

    Was it something you wanted before seeing the commercial? _____

    Did you need it?_____

    Was it worth the money? _____

    Was another brand available?_____

    Was it really as good as the commercial made it seem? Explain._____

    _____

7.  After reading this article, will you look at commercials differently? Explain.

    _____

    _____

    _____

Read the passage. Then, answer the questions.

# Superstitions

Have you ever avoided walking under a ladder because you thought it would bring you bad luck? If so, you were following a superstition. A superstition is a belief that if you do a certain thing, it will cause a totally different thing to happen. Superstitions have existed for hundreds of years. Most people today do not believe old superstitions, but they still follow them just to be safe!

There are superstitions that have to do with sleeping, working, eating, getting married, playing, and walking. It can be fun to learn about superstitions even if you don't believe in them.

Some superstitions predict good luck, such as throwing rice at a bride and groom, knocking on wood, finding a four-leaf clover, or carrying a rabbit's foot. Other superstitions warn of back luck, such as spilling salt, breaking a mirror, or having a black cat walk across your path. Superstitions can be fun to learn about. What do you think of superstitions?

1. The author thinks superstitions are _____.

   A. good luck

   B. bad luck

   C. rules you can't break

   D. fun to learn about

2. According to the author, most people today _____.

   A. believe superstitions and follow them exactly

   B. do not believe superstitions but follow them anyway

   C. think superstitions predict the future

   D. think superstitions cause things to happen

3. Do you follow any superstitions? If you were going to write about superstitions, what would you say?

   _____

   _____

   _____

   _____

Name_____

Read each paragraph. Then, answer the questions.

# Samantha's Birthday

A.    I knew it would be a great day from the minute I woke up. Piled beside my bed was a stack of presents. I jumped out of bed. I was so excited. When I came downstairs carrying the presents, everyone shouted, "Happy Birthday!"

B.    Before Samantha woke up, I left her presents beside her bed. I knew she would like the surprise from her father and me. When we saw Samantha on the stairs, we surprised her by saying, "Happy Birthday!"

C.    I bought Samantha a book about dinosaurs for her birthday. Mom and Dad let me do extra chores to earn the money. I had to wake up early to surprise her but, it was worth it to see her face when we all said, "Happy Birthday!"

1.  Who is the writer of passage A?_____

    What special day is it for this person? _____

    _____

2.  Who is the writer of passage B? _____

    How do you know? _____

    _____

3.  Who is the writer of passage C? _____

    How do you know? _____

Name_____

Read each paragraph. Then, answer the questions.

# A Sad Tale

A.    I felt sorry for Jason when I saw him come in this morning. He looked so sad. When it was finally time for recess, I asked him to stay behind. Then he told me his problem. With one quick phone call, the problem was solved.

B.    I was in such a rush this morning that I forgot my lunch. Mom had packed extra cookies today. At recess, Ms. Wagner asked me what was wrong. Then, she made a phone call, and Mom soon brought my lunch.

C.    As soon as Jason left for the bus, I saw his lunch sitting on the counter. I had planned to bring it to school anyway, but I was glad that Ms. Wagner called. Jason was so happy to see those cookies again.

1.    Who is the writer of passage A?_____

    How does this person help? _____

2.    Who is the writer of passage B? _____

    What is this person's main problem? _____

3.    Who is the writer of passage C?_____

    How does this person help? _____

Read the passage. Then, answer the questions.

# Reading Goals

Mrs. Walker's students each filled out a reading goal sheet in September. In January, the students reviewed their goals and evaluated how they had done. They each wrote a summary for their parents.

Here is Maddie's goal sheet from September:

> Goal:    My reading level is 2.5.
>             I would like to be reading at 3.5 by January.
> My plan to reach my goal:
> 1.    I need to read at home 15 minutes before school.
> 2.    I need to read at home 20 minutes after school.
> 3.    I need to pay attention during reading.
> 4.    I need to make sure what I read makes sense.

This is what Maddie wrote as her evaluation:

I know I met my goal because I am now reading at level 3.75. I met my goal because I made a chart on a calendar and kept track of my reading. I read every day before school except the week I was sick. I did read at least 20 minutes every day after school. I borrowed books at my reading level from my teacher and practiced them at school and at home. I paid attention when I read and made sure what I read made sense. When it did not make sense, I read it again. I always paid attention during reading in class. I know I am doing better in reading because I can read harder books and because I really like reading now.

1.    Based on her evaluation, how does Maddie feel about her goal? _____

_____

Highlight details that make you believe this.

2.    How does Maddie's plan compare with her evaluation? _____

_____

3.    Name three things Maddie stated in her evaluation that helped her reach her goal.

_____

_____

Read the diary entries. Then, answer the questions.

# Visiting Grandparents

**Monday:** I arrived at Grandma and Grandpa's house. It was after supper, but I was hungry. Gramps made me a ham sandwich with potato chips. I have a bedroom all to myself. It has a full-sized bed with a blue and red quilt. One whole wall is full of bookshelves with books. I can't wait to read some of them. Maybe Gram will let me take some home with me. I can see a pond from the window. I wonder if there are any fish in it?

**Tuesday:** After breakfast, Gram took me to the pond. It is full of fish. We fed them bread crumbs and left-over pancakes. The fish eat more pancakes than I do! Too bad they couldn't enjoy Gramps's homemade maple syrup. A family of ducks came and ate too. One duck even took bread out of my hand.

**Wednesday:** We went shopping.

**Thursday:** Grandma and Grandpa took me to see the caves. They were really cool. In fact the temperature was cool too. It was really dark in the caves. We had to wear hats with lights on them. In the caves were gigantic stalactites and stalagmites. In one of the underground pools, I saw fish without eyes. I bought a postcard about the blind fish to send to Mom and Dad.

1.  Name one activity the author did not care for. _____

    How can you tell he did not like this activity? _____

    _____

2.  Name an activity the author liked._____

    What makes you believe the author liked this activity? _____

    _____

3.  Name another activity the author liked. _____

    What makes you believe the author liked this activity? _____

    _____

Read the passage. Then, answer the questions.

# Puzzles

Today Jan, William, Tony, and I cleaned up our classroom. We had indoor recess because it was raining outside. Boy, did everyone make a mess! Taylor had finished a puzzle, then left it on the counter. Then he played a game of checkers with Brian and left for the bathroom. We picked up the puzzle for him. Then, we washed the counter. That counter was very dirty! It sure looked nice when we were finished.

When Taylor came back, he was angry. He said he had wanted to show the puzzle to his teacher. I told him he should have picked it up or told everyone he was going to take care of it later.

After the counter, we cleaned up the sink area, the recess cupboard, the book area, and the math shelves. The room just sparkled. I think we did a better job than the janitor does! Our teacher was sure impressed. She said we could be the official class cleaners.

1.  How does the author feel about cleaning up the room? _____

    _____

    Highlight details that make you believe this.

2.  Does the author believe putting away the puzzle was right or wrong?

    _____

    What does she write that makes you believe this? _____

    _____

3.  Does Taylor believe putting away the puzzle was right or wrong?_____

    What makes you believe this?_____

    _____

Read the letter. Then, answer the questions on page 75.

# Letter to Grandma

Dear Grandma,

    I am glad that you are having a good time on the beach. I'll bet it is warm there. Are you too hot? Do you have to use fans and an air conditioner? I can't wait to get there during spring vacation. I want to go fishing with you and Grandpa and swim and pick up shells and walk on the beach.

    It is snowing like crazy here. Don't tell my mom I am telling you, but Mom cracked up the car yesterday. Some guy crashed right into the back of the car. It was just too icy. Mom was really upset. She even "cooked" at a restaurant on the way home. I hope she will pick up take-out food more often, even if the car is OK.

    I had fun in the snow. We have a huge sledding hill. Molly and I went down it over and over. We made a family of snowmen too. Then we got cold. My fingers and toes felt like they were going to fall right off! My snow pants were soaked right through and my nose and cheeks were redder than all get out.

    Hey, is your nose red? Are you wearing sunscreen on your face? Remember when you made me put some on and I cried because I was so little. I think Molly cried more than I did.

    I sure miss you. I will see you soon.

                  Love,
                  Ian

Use the letter on page 74 to answer the questions.

1. How does the author feel about how things are going where he lives?
   List two good things and two negative things about Ian's home.

   Good                                    Negative

   _____                  _____

   _____                  _____

2. What did Ian mean when he said his mother "cooked" at a restaurant?

   _____

   _____

   What words told you that? _____

   Does the author like it when his mom "cooks at a restaurant"? How do you know?

   _____

   _____

3. How does Ian feel about where his grandma is?
   List two good things and two negative things about Grandma's home.

   Good                                    Negative

   _____                  _____

   _____                  _____

Read the passage. Then, answer the questions.

# Lazy Time

Sally and Nick are swaying slowly in the family swing. The air is crisp. Sally puts her arm around Nick and snuggles into his shaggy body. Nick's tongue licks Sally's hand that lies on her blue-jean leg. They watch a sluggish ladybug crawl underneath a pile of old, brown leaves. One red leaf drifts to the top of the ladybug's leaf pile. Nick's graying ears stand up as a southbound V of geese honks goodbye. The sky slowly turns from blue, to pink, to purple, to black.

The first star shines as Sally's mom calls her in to eat. Sally gives a last push as she slides out of the swing. She walks to the back door of the house. Nick leaps down. He barks once at a rabbit, and then chases after Sally. She smiles and rubs Nick's head as they walk into the warm house together.

1. What time of year is it?

   A. summer

   B. autumn

   C. winter

   D. spring

2. What time of day is it?

   A. morning

   B. afternoon

   C. evening

   D. night

3. What meal is Sally's family going to eat?

   A. breakfast

   B. lunch

   C. snack

   D. supper

4. Where could this story take place?

   A. Florida

   B. Hawaii

   C. Wisconsin

   D. California

Read the passage. Then, answer the questions.

# Vasco de Balboa

Vasco de Balboa was born in Spain in 1475. As he grew up, he heard stories about Columbus discovering America. In 1501, Balboa left Spain and sailed to Hispaniola, an island near South America. He later left the island and traveled to a part of Central America called Darién. Balboa was made governor of Darién.

In 1513, Balboa left Darién to search for treasures. It was during this trip that Balboa discovered what we now call the Pacific Ocean.

Balboa was excited with his new discovery. But when he returned to Darién, he found that a new governor named Pedrarias had replaced him. Balboa moved to a different site and built a city. He built new ships for exploration and made many friends.

In 1518, Pedrarias accused Balboa of treason. Balboa was innocent, but he was arrested and jailed. Pedrarias sentenced Balboa to death.

1.  What effect do you think the stories Balboa heard about Columbus when he was young had on him?

    A.  They made him want to be an explorer.

    B.  They scared him.

    C.  They made him want to be a governor.

    D.  They angered him.

3.  What do you think Balboa is most famous for today?

    A.  being governor of Darién

    B.  discovering the Pacific Ocean

    C.  being jailed by Pedrarias

    D.  growing up in Spain

2.  Why do you think Balboa built a new city when he returned to Darién?

    A.  He wanted to fight Pedrarias.

    B.  He thought he should still be governor of Darién.

    C.  He decided not to fight Pedrarias.

    D.  He was interested in architecture.

Read the play. Then, answer the questions on page 79.

# On Stage

MR. BOYSON: (*shaking his finger at Abe*) How many times do I have to tell you to quit
doing that?

ABE: I can't help it! If I could lock them in a closet and leave them there, I could stop.

MR. BOYSON: Well, that would be odd. If you don't quit soon, your poor fingernails are
going to forget how to grow!

ABE: Hey, come on, Dad. I bet you did it when you were a kid.

MR. BOYSON: Never did.

ABE: By the way, when can we visit Sizzle?

MR. BOYSON: Sizzle may not even recognize us.

ABE: (*very surprised*) She'd never forget me!

MR. BOYSON: She may not want a visit. You know she'll
look different now.

ABE: I know she's expecting. (*getting excited*) Do you think
she'll have more than one?

MR. BOYSON: (*sitting down on the living room couch*)
Probably not. They usually have one at a time.

ABE: I can't wait to see it! (*walking behind the couch so his dad can't see him*) Poor
Sizzle. She hated it when we took her to the zoo.

MR. BOYSON: Yes, but later she only seemed to notice us when we brought her
bananas.

ABE: I don't blame her; we abandoned her! It was Uncle Jack's fault. (*biting his nails,
but walking in front of the couch*) I wanted to keep her!

MR. BOYSON: Now don't blame Jack. You were delighted when he brought her
home. (*sees Abe biting nails*) Abe! (*shouting*) How many times do I have to tell you
to stop doing that?

Use the play on page 78 to answer the questions.

1.  What is the relationship between Mr. Boyson and Abe?

    A.  brothers

    B.  father and son

    C.  uncle and nephew

    D.  teacher and student

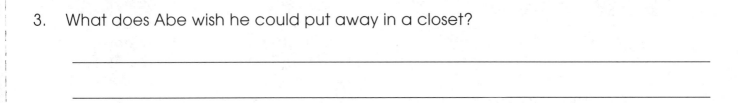

2.  What is the relationship between Abe and Jack?

    A.  brothers

    B.  father and son

    C.  uncle and nephew

    D.  teacher and student

3.  What does Abe wish he could put away in a closet?

    _____

    _____

4.  What do you know about Sizzle?

    _____

    _____

5.  Why wouldn't Sizzle want them to visit?

    _____

    _____

Read the article. Then, complete the activities on page 81.

# The Kansas Gazette

---

38th Year  **The Kansas Gazette**  April 2, 1900

---

## Cyclone Strikes Kansas

Yesterday, at exactly 3:38 pm, a huge cyclone spun out of control, causing great fear throughout the entire state.

A local farmer and his wife, Uncle Henry and Auntie Em, described seeing livestock and small pets flying through the air. Other unidentified objects were also seen flying through the sky.

Dozens of people were taken to area hospitals, including Henry's young niece, who was knocked unconscious by the flying objects.

Many houses were completely destroyed. Many of those still standing have been seriously damaged.

Those in authority cannot predict when order will be restored in the state or when the cleanup will be completed.

Although the situation is serious, there was one ray of hope. A beautiful rainbow appeared after the storm, promising happier times.

Name_____

Use the article on page 80 to complete the activities.

1. Check all of the correct answers.
   The reporter appears to be

   A. _____ knowledgeable about the incident

   B. _____ knowledgeable about how cyclones
          develop

   C. _____ hopeful about the future

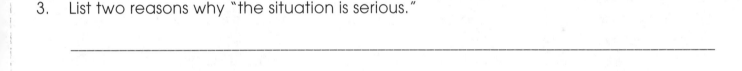

2. Circle the words that describe the reporter's reaction
   to the cyclone.

   unaffected        excited        unexpressive

   optimistic        indifferent        emotional

3. List two reasons why "the situation is serious."

   _____

   _____

4. Check each sentence that is a fact stated specifically in the newspaper article.

   A. _____ Many people were killed by the cyclone.

   B. _____ The reporter has seen many cyclones.

   C. _____ This was probably the largest cyclone to ever strike the state.

   D. _____ Cyclones often occur in Kansas.

   E. _____ The cleanup will take a long time.

   F. _____ Cyclones can lift heavy objects.

5. What do you think the name of the farmer's niece is? _____

   Why? _____

Read the passage. Then, answer the questions on page 83.

# Chocolate Bars

Do you like to eat chocolate candy bars? Your parents may not let you eat chocolate very often, but long ago, many children did not get to eat chocolate at all. In fact, before the 1900s, most Americans had never tasted chocolate.

In ancient times, as early as 1000 BC, people enjoyed chocolate in a drink. It was made from cocoa beans and spices. It was very bitter. Over time, people learned to add sugar to make the drink sweeter. It wasn't until 1828 that a Dutch chemist found a way to make the fine powder we know as cocoa. Soon, candy makers began to find ways to make candy from cocoa.

In 1875, Daniel Peter of the Swiss General Chocolate Company and Henri Nestlé found a way to produce milk chocolate. Making the milk chocolate took a lot of work and was very expensive. It also took a long time; it took a whole week to make one batch of milk chocolate. People loved the milk chocolate. Some people used it as a medicine for mental stress, sickness, and weakness.

In the early 1900s, Milton S. Hershey found a way to **mass produce** milk chocolate, or make it in large amounts, in a factory. He made the Hershey bars in his factory in Hershey, Pennsylvania. Mr. Hershey wanted everyone to be able to enjoy chocolate, so he sold his chocolate bars for five cents each. This was the first time most people could afford to eat and enjoy chocolate.

Thanks to these early scientists and the candy makers of today, we have been enjoying milk chocolate in many kinds of candy bars.

Use the passage on page 82 to answer the questions.

1.  Use one word to name the topic of this article. _____

    Highlight the first time you found this word in the article.

2.  Why do you think that most children did not get to eat milk chocolate before the early 1900s? _____

    _____

    _____

    Highlight details that helped you decide this.

3.  Do you think the milk chocolate made by Peter and Nestlé was expensive or inexpensive? _____

    What evidence does the article give to support your answer?

    _____

    _____

4.  What is the definition of **mass produce** in this article? _____

    _____

    Highlight where you found the answer.

5.  Why was Milton Hershey important to the history of milk chocolate?_____

    _____

    _____

    Highlight the details that helped you decide this.

6.  Were chocolate candy bars available in 1000 BC? _____

    What evidence does the article give to support your answer? _____

    _____

    _____

7.  What is your favorite candy bar? _____

Read the passage. Then, answer the questions.

# The North Star

The North Star is one of the most famous stars. Its star name is Polaris. It is called the North Star because it shines almost directly over the North Pole. If you are at the North Pole, the North Star is overhead. As you travel farther south, the star seems lower in the sky. Only people in the Northern Hemisphere can see the North Star.

Because the North Star is always in the same spot in the sky, it has been used for years to give direction to people at night. Sailors used the North Star to navigate through the oceans.

Polaris, like all stars, is always moving. Thousands of years from now, another star will get to be the North Star. Vega was the North Star thousands of years before it moved out of position and Polaris became the North Star.

1. The North Star might be one of the most famous stars because _____.

   A. it is near the North Pole

   B. it is always moving

   C. it is always in the same spot in the sky

   D. it is difficult to find in the sky

2. Another star will someday get to be the North Star because _____.

   A. stars are always moving

   B. there are many stars in the sky

   C. Earth will turn to the South Pole

   D. scientists rename the North Star every 50 years

3. The name Polaris most likely comes from which name?

   A. polecat

   B. polar bear

   C. Poland

   D. North Pole

4. Only people in the _____ Hemisphere can see the North Star.

   A. Northern

   B. Southern

   C. Western

   D. Eastern

Read the passage. Then, answer the questions.

# Venus Flytrap

Kayla got a Venus flytrap for her birthday. She put it with her other plants on her windowsill. She watered all of her plants each day.

After a week, all of her plants looked fine except for her gift. She decided that she needed more information on this plant, so she went to the library and found a book about the Venus flytrap.

She was surprised to find out that this plant is **carnivorous**, or meat-eating. No wonder it was not doing well! The book said that the Venus flytrap is a popular house plant. Each set of leaves stays open until an insect or piece of meat lands on the inside of the leaf. The two leaves close quickly, trapping the bait inside. After a leaf digests the meat, it dies. A new leaf grows to take the place of the dead leaf.

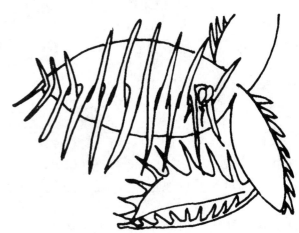

1.  What kind of plant did Kayla get for her birthday? _____

2.  Why did Kayla decide to go to the library?_____

    _____

3.  What information about the plant surprised Kayla? _____

    _____

4.  What does the word **carnivorous** mean? _____

5.  What do you predict Kayla will do next? Highlight important details in the text that helped you with your prediction.

    _____

    _____

    _____

    _____

Read the passage. Then, answer the questions.

# Opera

What do you think of when you hear the word *opera*? Do you think of singing, fancy costumes, and orchestra music? Opera is all of those things and more! Opera is a <u>play in which the actors sing</u> most of their lines.

An opera is made up of two parts—the libretto and the music. The libretto is the <u>story or words of an opera</u>. Many people read the libretto of an opera before they see the performance. This helps them follow the story as it is sung. The music of an opera <u>includes the singers, the orchestra, and the conductor</u>. An opera singer must be an excellent singer, an actor, and sometimes a dancer as well. The orchestra provides the background music for the entire opera. And the conductor has the job of <u>keeping the singers and the orchestra on beat and working together</u>.

Look at the underlined phrases in the passage. Decide what is being described by the phrase by noticing the words around it.

1.  To what does a <u>play in which the actors sing</u> refer?

    A.  music

    B.  dancers

    C.  actors

    D.  opera

2.  To what does <u>the story or words of an opera</u> refer?

    A.  singers

    B.  actors

    C.  libretto

    D.  orchestra

3.  What <u>includes the singers, the orchestra, and the conductor</u>?

    A.  music

    B.  opera

    C.  libretto

    D.  background

4.  Who has the job of <u>keeping the singers and the orchestra on beat and working together</u>?

    A.  actors

    B.  conductor

    C.  dancers

    D.  singers

Read the passage. Then, answer the questions.

# Braille

Braille is a special system that <u>makes it possible for blind people to read</u> by touching a book. It is a code of dots raised on the paper.

Braille was developed in 1829 by Louis Braille, a 15-year-old blind student in France. His code is still used today.

Braille code is made from six dots. The dots are placed two across and three down. From these six dots, many different symbols can be made <u>by raising certain dots</u>. This six-dot code can make the alphabet, numerals, punctuation marks, and more.

The metal plates for making braille material first have the dotted code placed on them and then are <u>pressed against paper</u>. This forms the dotted code on the paper. Books, magazines, and even menus are written in Braille.

Look at the underlined phrases in the passage. Decide what is being described by the phrase by noticing the words around it.

1. To what does <u>makes it possible for blind people to read</u> refer?

   A. touch

   B. book

   C. Braille

   D. paper

2. What can be made <u>by raising certain dots</u>?

   A. texture

   B. drawings

   C. many different symbols

   D. metal plates

3. What is <u>pressed against paper</u>?

   A. magazines

   B. metal plates

   C. books

   D. Braille

4. Write at least two examples from the text of items that have been written in Braille.

   _____

   _____

   _____

   _____

Choose the best meaning for the underlined word as used in the sentence.

# A Switch Is a Switch

1. As Myra walked out of the room, she turned the <u>switch</u> to off and the light went out.

   A. to change from one thing to another

   B. something used to turn off and on lights

   C. a slender, flexible rod or twig

2. Dad told the children that they should have <u>minded</u> him. If they had, the bikes would not have been stolen.

   A. something you think with

   B. to dig minerals out of the earth

   C. to follow someone's directions

3. Jenna carefully removed the wax from the <u>mold</u>. Each candle was shaped like a star.

   A. a form for making something into a certain shape

   B. a fuzzy growth

   C. the surface of the earth

4. Dolphins, sharks, and fish are all <u>aquatic</u> animals.

   A. live on land

   B. eat meat

   C. live in the water

5. Mom put a little <u>pat</u> of butter on the side of the plate.

   A. to gently pet or tap

   B. someone's name

   C. a small, individual portion

An idiom is a figure of speech. The meaning of an idiom is something different from what the words actually say. After each sentence, write **X** in front of the best meaning for the underlined idiom.

# Figure It Out

1. Ginny has a beautiful flower garden. It seems like everything she plants grows. She really has <u>a green thumb</u>.

   _____ Ginny's thumb is green in color.

   _____ Ginny is a good gardener.

   _____ Ginny has a green leaf wrapped around her thumb.

2. The storm came quickly and the rain poured down hard. Soon, three inches of rain had fallen. Tom said it was <u>raining cats and dogs</u>.

   _____ It was raining really hard.

   _____ Cats and dogs were running around in the rain.

   _____ Cats and dogs were falling from the sky.

3. Patrick and Tara have a new puppy. All day they chased him around the yard. They are ready to drop. The puppy <u>ran them ragged</u>.

   _____ The puppy tore their clothes into rags.

   _____ Patrick and Tara used a rag to play with the puppy.

   _____ The puppy made Patrick and Tara very tired.

4. Ruby <u>couldn't keep a straight face</u>. The kittens were so funny. They chased each other's tails and got tangled up in Ruby's shoelaces.

   _____ Ruby couldn't look at the kittens.

   _____ Ruby was angry at the kittens for scratching her face.

   _____ Ruby just had to smile.

Read each paragraph on page 90 and 91. Look at the underlined figure of speech. Write **X** in front of the best meaning for the underlined idiom.

# What Does It Mean?

1.     Joe and Grace needed information for their report on theropods. It was hard to find resources on this dinosaur. They decided not to get another topic. They would <u>leave no stone unturned</u> while looking for information.

_____ They would look for information everywhere.

_____ They planned to turn over a lot of stones on the playground.

_____ They would look under many things.

2.     Hugo was out of ideas. He decided that <u>two heads are better than one</u>. He asked his friend Olner to help him with his problem-solving assignment.

_____ Looking at two heads is better than looking at one.

_____ Two people thinking together come up with better ideas than one person can by himself.

_____ Two of anything is better than one.

3.     The teacher walked down the hallway to get a new pack of pencils. While he was gone, his students ran around the room, yelled, and threw paper wads. He walked back in and said, "<u>When the cat's away, the mice will play</u>."

_____ Mice play with the cat's toys when the cat is gone.

_____ People don't behave as well when the person in charge is gone.

_____ Cats like to eat mice.

4.     Sally got her hamburger and fries. Then she saw her friend Patsy had a chicken sandwich with a chocolate shake. Sally wished she had gotten what Patsy had. She asked Patsy if she wanted to trade. "No," said Patsy. "You know the grass is always greener on the other side of the fence."

_____ What someone else has always looks better.

_____ If you water your grass as much as your neighbor does, you will have green grass too.

_____ The way the light shines on the other side of a fence makes the grass look greener.

5.     Bill hit a baseball through the window. When his dad asked him how it happened, he lied and said his sister had done it. His dad had seen him do it. Now he was out of the frying pan and into the fire.

_____ The baseball had fallen into a frying pan and then bounced into the fireplace.

_____ Frying pans usually sit on top of fire, so you have to be careful not to spill things.

_____ Bill was in more trouble now than he had been to start with.

6.     Rebecca didn't finish her math homework last night. She played on the computer instead. She asked her mother to tell her teacher that she had been sick. Her mother told her that she would have to face the music herself.

_____ When you play the piano, you must look at the music sheets.

_____ Her teacher would ask her a musical question.

_____ Rebecca must be honest with her teacher and accept the consequences.

Read the letter. Then, complete the activity.

# What a Trip!

Dear <u>Mom</u> (1),

    <u>Dad</u> (2) and I are having a <u>miserable</u> (3) time visiting <u>Uncle</u> (4) Jenny. We are <u>asleep</u> (5) every <u>evening</u> (6) at six o'clock to get a <u>late</u> (7) start sightseeing.

    Yesterday, we <u>came</u> (8) to a museum. It contained <u>modern</u> (9) artifacts from an Egyptian tomb. The museum was <u>empty</u> (10) with <u>cheap</u> (11) objects. A mummy's mask was solid <u>silver</u> (12). It was an <u>ordinary</u> (13) sight!

    So far, <u>nothing</u> (14) we've done has been <u>boring</u> (15).

Your <u>son</u> (16),

Kim

1. Each underlined word is incorrect. An antonym (opposite) for each word should have been used. Write the number of each word on the line by the correct antonym.

_____ priceless      _____ gold      _____ Aunt      _____ filled

_____ awake      _____ Mom      _____ wonderful      _____ extraordinary

_____ Dad      _____ exciting      _____ everything      _____ went

_____ ancient      _____ early      _____ daughter      _____ morning

Read the passage. Then, complete the activity.

# The Great Ice Age

Long ago, the climate of Earth began to cool. As the temperature dropped, giant sheets of ice, called glaciers, moved across the land. As time went on, snow and ice covered many forests and grasslands.

Some plants and animals could not survive the changes in the climate. Other animals moved to warmer land. But some animals were able to adapt. They learned to live with the cold and snowy weather.

Finally, Earth's temperature began to rise. The ice and snow began to melt. Today, the land at the North and South Poles is a reminder of the Great Ice Age.

For each pair of words or phrases, write **S** if they are synonyms or an **A** if they are antonyms.

1. _____ melt          freeze          6. _____ survive         die

2. _____ climate       weather         7. _____ dropped         fell

3. _____ adapt         change          8. _____ grasslands      prairie

4. _____ rise          fall            9. _____ remind          forget

5. _____ giant sheet   glacier         10. _____ temperature    measure of
          of ice                                                    heat or cold

Read the passage. Then, complete the activity.

# Coins

Coins are made in factories called **mints**. The first mint in America was in Philadelphia. Plans for this mint were started by a resolution of Congress on April 2, 1792. The first coins **struck**, or made, in America were minted that same year. The first **denomination** was called a half-disme or half-dime. A year later, several other denominations of coins were struck, including the quarter-dollar, the disme or dime, the gold eagle (worth $10), and the copper cent. It took a lot of work to mint coins. Before a coin could be manufactured, a die was made. In the late 1800s, these dies were cut by hand. First, an exact drawing had to be made. Then, the drawing was traced into wax. The wax was used as a pattern to shape the die. Finally a **die**, or mold, was finished which could be used to strike coins. Since this work was done by hand, the coins had small differences each time a new die was made.

Today, coins are **standardized**. Although hundreds of dies are used each year to make a denomination of coins, each die is made from the master die. Machines and computers are also used in this process so that the minted coins look alike. The only differences are the dates and the location codes that show where each coin was made.

Circle the correct answer.

1.  What is the meaning of the word **mint** as used in this passage?

    A. a piece of candy     B. a factory where coins are made     C. a lot of money

2.  What is the meaning of the word **struck** as used in this passage?

    A. to cross out     B.  to attack     C.  to make by stamping

3.  What is the meaning of the word **die** as used in this passage?

    A.  a mold     B.  to color with a stain or paint     C.  to stop living

4.  What is the meaning of the word **standardized** as used in this passage?

    A.  original     B.  the same every time     C.  a flag

5.  What is the meaning of the word **denomination** as used in this passage?

    A.  having the same size and value     B.  color     C.  sharing the same beliefs

Name_____

Read the passage. Then, complete the activity.

# A Black Hole

Have you ever heard of a black hole? Some scientists believe that a black hole is a mysterious object somewhere in space that you cannot see. The scientists believe that it has such a strong pull toward it that nothing can escape from it.

Some scientists believe that a black hole is a star that collapsed. The collapse made its pull even stronger. It seems invisible because even its own starlight cannot escape. It is believed that anything in space that comes near the black hole will soar into it and disappear forever.

Most black holes weigh as much as a giant star. A typical black hole could have a mass ten times that of the sun. Some scientists believe our whole galaxy is full of black holes.

For each sentence, circle the word that is used the same way as in the passage.

1.  There are many mysteries of space that we cannot (see, sea).

2.  If a cow could fly into space, the (hole, whole) thing would disappear into a black hole.

3.  Someday I would like to (sore, soar) through space and study the galaxy.

4.  We cannot tell exactly what a giant star might (way, weigh).

5.  Earth's (sun, son) is a star that has not collapsed.

Read the passage. Then, complete the activities on page 97.

# Is Seeing Really Believing?

A magician may seem to have amazing powers, but most tricks are based on scientific techniques that fool the eyes. The magician is an actor who distracts the audience so he or she can do things unnoticed.

One type of magic trick is called sleight-of-hand. The illustrations on this page show a magician doing a **sleight-of-hand** trick. The magician makes it look as though one ball transforms into two balls. This trick requires a rubber ball and a special metal half-shell that looks like a ball. When the two are put together, the audience sees only one ball. Secretly, the magician separates the shell from the ball. Then, holding up the rubber ball and showing the half-shell from the front, it looks as though two balls have appeared. A magician's fingers must be very coordinated to do this trick.

**Illusionists** perform tricks using elaborate equipment. This is a second type of magic trick. An illusionist tries to make the audience believe that they see one thing when they actually see another. One famous illusion is sawing a person in half.

Another type of magic is **escape magic**. Escape magicians are able to free themselves from police handcuffs, leg irons, and locked jail cells. Escape magicians must be coordinated and physically fit to perform their tricks.

People love magic because they enjoy trying to figure out how magicians perform their tricks. However, magicians rarely reveal their secrets. They use carefully planned actions and words to get an audience to focus its attention on the wrong place at the right time.

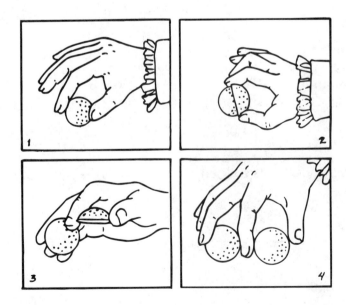

Name_____

Use the passage on page 96 to complete the activities.

1. Read the term from the passage in the first column. Write **S** on the line in front of its synonym and **A** in front of its antonym.

   A. distract        ___ laugh      ___ divert      ___ far        ___ attract

   B. transform       ___ change     ___ disappear   ___ let be     ___ cut

   C. coordinated     ___ clumsy     ___ graceful    ___ blind      ___ sleepy

   D. illusion        ___ person     ___ saw         ___ trick      ___ truth

2. Explain what the author meant by "They . . . get an audience to focus its attention on the wrong place at the right time."

   _____

   _____

3. Describe the three types of magic discussed in the passage.

   _____

   _____

   _____

4. Read each sentence. Write **T** if it is true or **F** if it is false.

   _____ A. Magicians try to get the audience to notice every movement.

   _____ B. The ball trick shown in the illustration really only uses one ball.

   _____ C. Some magicians use scientific techniques.

   _____ D. All magicians must be physically fit and well coordinated.

Read the passage. Then, complete the activity.

# Food for Thought

A waiter was taking a break. He said to a brand-new employee, "You just have to be the one to break the ice with the chef. Sometimes it seems like he has a chip on his shoulder, but he's okay. This is a busy place. You've jumped out of the frying pan and into the fire, let me tell you. I hope you don't have any pie-in-the-sky ideas about taking things easy here. Some days, I feel like I'm going bananas. It might not be your cup of tea. I think we've got the cream of the crop here; everybody does a great job. It's hard sometimes not to fly off the handle when things are so hectic, though. I think you'll do all right if you don't mind hard work."

Match each idiom with its meaning.

1. _____ to break the ice                 A.   unrealistic

2. _____ a chip on his shoulder           B.   something one enjoys

3. _____ out of the frying pan            C.   the best available
           and into the fire

4. _____ pie-in-the-sky                   D.   to make a start

5. _____ going bananas                    E.   to lose one's temper

6. _____ your cup of tea                  F.   seemingly angry or resentful

7. _____ the cream of the crop            G.   go crazy

8. _____ fly off the handle               H.   from a bad situation to a worse one

Read the passage. Then, answer the questions.

# Votes for Women

Elizabeth Cady Stanton was born in 1815. Her parents were important people and gave their daughter a complete education. She married anti-slavery speaker Henry Stanton in 1840.

Along with Lucretia Mott, Stanton helped to organize the 1848 Women's Rights Convention at Seneca Falls, New York. She became friends with Susan B. Anthony soon after this, and the two remained friends throughout their lives. Stanton became a popular speaker throughout the United States after the Civil War. She spoke about social reform issues.

Near the end of her life, Elizabeth Cady Stanton worked on a three-volume book called *History of Women's Suffrage*. After devoting most of her life to fighting for women's suffrage, Elizabeth Cady Stanton died 18 years before the passage of the Nineteenth Amendment, which finally gave women the right to vote.

1.  This passage is which genre (type) of literature?

    A.  poetry

    B.  fiction

    C.  biography

    D.  fable

2.  What clues in the story helped you decide what genre it is?

    _____

    _____

3.  Using the passage as an example, write a definition of this genre. Use the sentences below as a guide.

    _____ are usually about _____.

    _____ include details about _____.

Read the passage. Then, answer the questions.

# The Fox and the Grapes

One warm summer day, a fox was walking along when he noticed a bunch of grapes on a vine above him. Cool, juicy grapes would taste so good. The more he thought about it, the more the fox wanted those grapes.

He tried standing on his tiptoes. He tried jumping high in the air. He tried getting a running start before he jumped. But no matter what he tried, the fox could not reach the grapes.

As he angrily walked away, the fox muttered, "They were probably sour anyway!"

Moral:
A person (or fox) sometimes pretends that he does not want something he cannot have.

1. This passage is which genre (type) of literature?

   A. poetry

   B. biography

   C. nonfiction

   D. fable

2. What clues in the story helped you decide what genre it is?

   _____

   _____

3. Using the passage as an example, write a definition of this genre. Use the sentences below as a guide.

   _____ are usually about _____.

   _____ includes details about _____.

Read the poem. Then, complete the activities.

# Polar Bears

With fur like a snowstorm
And eyes like the night,
Two giant old bears
Sure gave me a fright.

They came up behind me
As quiet as mice,
And tapped on my shoulder.
Their paws were like ice.

As high as a kite,
I jumped in the air,
And turned round to see
Those bears standing there.

"We're sorry we scared you,"
The bears said so cool.
"We just came to ask you
To fill up our pool!"

Fill in the blanks to complete the similes from the poem. Then, write your own similes, comparing two things by using the words **like** or **as**.

1. paws **like** _____

2. fur **like** _____

3. **as** high **as** a _____

4. eyes **like** _____

5. **as** quiet **as** _____

6. _____

    _____

7. _____

    _____

8. _____

    _____

Read the poem. Then, answer the questions.

# My Backpack

My backpack's so heavy
It must weigh a ton.
With thousands of books
My work's never done.

My arms are so sore
I can't lift a pen.
My breath is so short
I need oxygen.

When I stoop over,
It makes me fall down.
I think I'll just stay here
All squashed on the ground.

1. Which of the following phrases is an example of **hyperbole** (exaggeration)?

   A. It makes me fall down

   B. My work's never done

   C. My breath is so short

   D. It must weigh a ton

2. The author decided there were too many exaggerations in the poem. Which of the following revised lines still contains a **hyperbole**?

   A. My backpack is so heavy, it's hard to lift.

   B. My arms are so sore, I can't lift a hen.

   C. With four small textbooks, my work's almost done.

   D. My breath is so short, I need to rest.

3. Write your own **hyperboles**. Remember that you should include exaggeration as part of your description.

   My dog is so ugly,

   _____

   _____

   I am so tired,

   _____

   _____

   I am so hungry,

   _____

   _____

Read the passage. Then, answer the questions.

# Black Beauty

Paraphrased from *Black Beauty* by Anna Sewell (Random House, 2000)

One day, when there was a good deal of kicking in the meadow, my mother whinnied to me to come to her. "I wish you to pay attention to what I am about to say. The colts who live here are very good colts, but they are cart-horse colts, and, of course, they have not learned manners. You have been well-bred and wellborn; your father has a great name in these parts. Your grandfather won the cup two years in a row at the Newmarket Races; your grandmother had the sweetest temper of any horse I have ever known. I think you have never seen me kick or bite. I hope you will grow up gentle and good and never follow bad ways. Do your work with goodwill, lift your legs up high when you trot, and never kick or bite, even in play."

1.  What did Black Beauty's mother say about each of his family members to prove he was "well-bred and wellborn"?

    A.  His father: _____

    B.  His grandfather: _____

    C.  His grandmother: _____

    D.  His mother: _____

2.  In your own words, write what you think "well-bred and wellborn" means.

    _____

    _____

3.  Select the word that best describes the attitude of Black Beauty's mother.

    A.  proud

    B.  angry

    C.  stingy

    D.  carefree

Read the passage. Then, answer the questions on page 105.

# Through the Looking Glass

From *Through the Looking Glass* by Lewis Carroll (Random House, 2002)

"She can't do Subtraction," said the White Queen. "Can you do Division? Divide a loaf by a knife. What's the answer to that?"

"I suppose—" Alice was beginning, but the Red Queen answered for her. "Bread-and-Butter, of course. Try another Subtraction sum. Take a bone from a dog: what remains?"

Alice considered. "The bone wouldn't remain, of course, if I took it— and the dog wouldn't remain; it would come to bite me, and I'm sure I shouldn't remain!"

"Then you think nothing would remain?" said the Red Queen.

"I think that's the answer."

"Wrong, as usual," said the Red Queen: "The dog's temper would remain."

"But, I don't see how—"

"Why, look here!" the Red Queen cried. "The dog would lose its temper, wouldn't it?"

"Perhaps it would," Alice replied cautiously.

"Then if the dog went away, its temper would remain!" the Queen exclaimed triumphantly.

Alice said, as gravely as she could, "They might go different ways." But she couldn't help thinking to herself, "What dreadful nonsense we ARE talking!"

Here the Red Queen began again. "Can you answer useful questions?" she said. "How is bread made?"

"I know THAT!" Alice cried eagerly. "You take some flour—"

"Where do you pick the flower?" the White Queen asked. "In a garden or in the hedges?"

"Well, it isn't PICKED at all," Alice explained: "it's GROUND."

"How many acres of ground?" said the White Queen. "You mustn't leave out so many things."

"Fan her head!" the Red Queen anxiously interrupted. "She'll be feverish after so much thinking."

Use the passage on page 104 to answer the questions.

1. Which word tells how Alice might be feeling by the end of the passage?

   A. hopeful

   B. proud

   C. frustrated

   D. excited

2. Which word tells how the Red Queen and the White Queen might be feeling by the end of the passage?

   A. sorry

   B. frustrated

   C. sad

   D. shy

3. Describe each character with two words.

   Red Queen _____

   _____

   White Queen_____

   _____

   Alice _____

   _____

4. Words that sound the same but have different meanings are called homonyms. Which **homonyms** does the White Queen use at the end of the story?

   A. whether, weather

   B. pail, pale

   C. write, right

   D. flour, flower

5. Answer the following question with an imaginary dialogue between the queens and Alice. How do you make pizza? Words to consider: *dough, flour, ham, cheese.*

   _____

   _____

   _____

   _____

   _____

   _____

   _____

   _____

   _____

   _____

   _____

Read the passage. Then, answer the questions.

# Ralph

Ralph was a dirty mutt. His once-white hair was gray and brown with grime. He wore a black collar around his neck that had once been blue. On the dirty collar hung an identification tag, if anyone could get close enough to read it.

Right now, Ralph was on his belly. He inched forward under the lilac bushes. His long hair dragged in the dirt. His bright, black eyes were glued on a plate at the edge of the table. On it was a ham sandwich. His moist, black nose twitched with the smell. Ralph knew he would get a stern scolding or spray with the hose if the lady of the house caught him in the yard again.

His empty belly made him brave. The screen door slammed as the lady went back for other goodies. Ralph knew it was time. He flew like a bullet to the edge of the table. The corner of the plate was in his mouth long enough to tip it onto the ground. Ralph's teeth seized the sandwich and he was off. The door slammed, and a yell was heard. As he dove through a hole in the bushes, water from the hose whitened the back half of his body and his dirty tail.

1. What is Ralph? _____

   Highlight the details that helped you decide this.

2. Is Ralph living in a home with people the day he steals the sandwich? _____

   Highlight the details that helped you decide this.

3. Did Ralph have a home with people at one time?_____

   _____

   Highlight the details that helped you decide this.

4. How does the lady in the passage feel about Ralph? _____

   What details cause you to think this? _____

   _____

5. Draw Ralph in the frame above. Each time you draw a detail, highlight it in the text.

Read each paragraph. Then, use the word bank to choose the setting for each one.

# Times and Travels

| Egyptian Desert | Ancient Rome | Medieval England |
| Winter | Mother's Day |

1.  Ella still had a mile to walk to school, and her boots were already wet. The shawl her mother had wrapped over her patched coat was not keeping her warm.

Setting: _____

2.  "There they are, son," Jacob's father said quietly. Jacob's eyes widened. He forgot about the long trip, the blazing sun, and even the camel ride. Nothing mattered except these vast pyramids of stone.

Setting: _____

3.  Rachel ran down the stairs clutching a big, white envelope. She could smell the pancakes Dad flipped in the pan. "Oh, good," she sighed, walking into the empty dining room. "I wanted to put this on Mom's plate before she came down to breakfast."

Setting: _____

4.  Casey picked up his helmet as Christopher held the heavy lance. "This joust will be attended by the king," Casey told his page. "If I do well, I may gain the favor of His Majesty."

Setting: _____

5.  Marcus stopped and smoothed down the folds of his toga before entering the Roman temple. He stopped again as he saw Augustus, the new senator, stride up the steps before him.

Setting: _____

Read each paragraph. Circle the word that tells when it happened. Highlight the key word or words that helped you decide.

# Now or Later

1.    In 1492, it was widely believed that monsters lived in the oceans. Travelers worried that their ship would be eaten or sunk before they got where they wanted to go.

    past         present         future

2.    Jamie is working on an art project. The background is colored with crayon and he is putting a wash of paint over the top.

    past         present         future

3.    It is hot! It is so hot that the ice in Tiffany's glass melts before she can drink it. The swing is hanging limply with no one in it. Butch, the dog, is sprawled in the shade with his tongue hanging out. Tiffany moves the sprinkler into the shade and turns it on.

    past         present         future

4.    Tia and Leo are on their way to grandmother's house. The trip from Jupiter to Earth takes two hours. They haven't been to Earth in a month and they look forward to swimming in the ocean.

    past         present         future

5.    The 74-foot-long Brachiosaurus stretched its neck to reach the leaves at the top of the tree. It ripped off a mouthful and munched slowly.

    past         present         future

6.    Anna, 50 years old, tells her granddaughter about third grade. "Back around the year 2000, we were just beginning to use computers in all of the classrooms."

    past         present         future

Read the passage. Then, answer the questions.

# Decision

    The birds are chirping. Little green leaves are just beginning to form on the branches of the trees. Crocuses and early spring flowers bring color to the downtown yards. A gentle breeze whispers of warm weather. Heath is walking slowly with his head down. He does not notice any of the morning's beauty. He has to decide what to do.

    Heath's best friend, Shane, wants them to skip school today. Shane has big plans for the day. Shane wants to do daring things. Heath really likes Shane. They are great friends. Heath doesn't want to hurt Shane's feelings or for Shane to think he is a chicken. Still, Heath knows it is wrong to skip school. Heath knows he can get into a world of trouble—at home and at school. And trouble at home would make the school trouble look like a party. Heath suddenly knows what his decision has to be.

1. When does the story take place?_____

2. Where does the story take place?_____

3. Who are the characters?_____

_____

4. What is the problem?_____

_____

5. How do you predict the problem will be solved?_____

_____

_____

Highlight the details that helped you decide this.

Read the passage. Then, answer the questions.

# Water's Edge

Gabe walked down to the water. The sun was setting. The sky was blazing with oranges, yellow, pinks, and reds. The tide was coming in. At the edge of the water was an odd-looking creature about one foot long. Its body seemed to be in three parts. The first part was about three-fourths of a hemisphere. Fitting into the hemisphere was a smaller body part with jagged edges. A long, hard, pointed tail poked its way out of the smaller body part. "What is that thing?" wondered Gabe. "Can it hurt me?"

He saw Hannah walking toward him on the beach and called her over. "Do you know what this is?" he asked.

"It's a horseshoe crab," replied Hannah. "My older sister studies them. She knows a lot about horseshoe crabs."

"Great," said Gabe. "I want to know more about them."

1.  When does the story take place? _____

2.  Where does the story take place? _____

3.  Who are the characters?_____

    _____

4.  What is the problem?_____

    _____

5.  How do you predict the problem will be solved? _____

    _____

    _____

    Highlight the details that helped you decide this.

Read the passage. Then, complete the activity.

# Power's Out

When a severe storm comes, you may lose electrical power. There are things you can do to prepare for a power outage.

First of all, you need a non-electrical light source, such as a flashlight, lantern, or candles. Make sure you have fresh batteries, fuel for the lantern, or matches for the candles. A battery-powered radio will help you get weather and emergency information. It is a good idea to unplug equipment, such as answering machines, computers, televisions, and microwaves. Lightning strikes or power surges can damage these items.

If a storm is coming that may cause the power to be out for more than just a few hours, you will want to prepare some other items. Fill empty milk jugs with fresh water if you have an electric well for water. Use the jugs of water for drinking, cooking over a camp stove, and flushing toilets. Keep healthy foods on hand that can be prepared and eaten without the use of electricity, such as fruit, bread, and peanut butter. If you live in an area with cold weather, you will need a plan to keep warm. Even if you have gas heat, most furnaces have electric starters. Find extra blankets or purchase a generator with gasoline to run the furnace.

Being prepared for a power outage can make the difference between a serious problem and a cozy family experience.

I.  Use the information in the passage to write the solution to each problem. Highlight where you found the information in the text.

| Problem | Solution |
|---|---|
| The television is out and you cannot listen to the news for information about the storm. | |
| The well has stopped working so you cannot flush the toilet. | |
| The furnace will not start and it is getting very cold in the house. | |
| You are hungry and your electric stove does not work. | |
| The power is out and it is dark in the house. | |

Read the passage. Then, answer the questions on page 113.

# The Thief of Sherwood Forest

The Sheriff of Nottingham sighed. He looked at me sadly. "Will, I fear there has been another robbery," he said. "Prince John will want to know why."

I was only a page, but I felt proud when the Sheriff talked to me about his troubles. I unfolded his napkin and asked, "My lord, when did this crime take place?"

"It was yesterday as the taxes were taken by wagon out of the gates of the city. This thief of the forest took all the money!" Now the Sheriff looked worried. "Prince John will want his money, whether it has been collected already or not. He may ask everyone to pay their taxes again. Many cannot afford to do that."

I nodded, trying to look wise and grown up. "Maybe you could ask Prince John for mercy, my lord," I said.

The Sheriff sighed again, though he tried to smile at me. "I could, Will. I could try. But Prince John is angry that I have not been able to catch this thief. If only Sherwood Forest were not so large! It is as if he simply disappears in the woods."

"Some people in town are saying that this thief gives the money back to them," I told my master.

"I know, Will, I know. But he does not give back nearly as much as he takes. We have proof of that. This thief grows rich, and the people grow only a little less poor."

"Still," I answered as I served the Sheriff some soup, "the stories have made this thief well liked. People may hope that he will give them back these taxes too."

Now the Sheriff's face looked stern. "Those taxes belong to Prince John," he said. "That is the law. Good people obey the laws. They know that this robber must be stopped. I am sure they do."

I silently spooned potatoes onto a plate. I knew better. The stories were more powerful than my master would admit. The thief from the forest was using these tales to make himself harder to catch.

I feared that very few people in town would help my master and his soldiers in the task that lay ahead of them.

Use the passage on page 112 to answer the questions.

1. The story is told by _____.

   A. a thief in the forest

   B. the Sheriff of Nottingham

   C. a page named Will

   D. the King

2. Who is the thief in the story?

   A. Robin Hood

   B. Friar Tuck

   C. the Sheriff of Nottingham

   D. Will

3. What is the Sheriff's main problem in this story?

   A. He needs to pay his own taxes to Prince John.

   B. He needs to get back the tax money that has been stolen.

   C. He needs to make sure people know the truth about the thief.

   D. He needs to hire people to catch the thief.

4. How is this story different from a story told from Robin Hood's point of view?

   A. The story points out that Robin Hood was very popular.

   B. The story shows the trouble that Robin Hood was making for law-abiding people.

   C. The story shows that Robin Hood was robbing people of money.

   D. The story shows the Sheriff of Nottingham was a villain.

5. What does Will understand that his master, the Sheriff, does not?

   A. Robin Hood is really a good person.

   B. Robin Hood is using the forest as a place to hide.

   C. Robin Hood's stories have made him so popular that people may not help the Sheriff.

   D. Everyone will want to help the Sheriff catch Robin Hood.

Read the chart. Then, complete the activity.

# Pencils

Mrs. Santo's class needs to buy new pencils. They decided to test four different kinds. They recorded their findings in a chart.

| Brand | Lasted for one week or longer | Kept a sharp point | Eraser lasted for one week or longer | Eraser worked well |
|-------|-------------------------------|--------------------|--------------------------------------|--------------------|
| Brand A | no | no | yes | no |
| Brand B | yes | yes | no | yes |
| Brand C | no | yes | no | yes |
| Brand D | yes | yes | yes | no |

Read each sentence. Using information from the chart, write **T** if it is true or **F** is it is false.

1. _____ Brand B lasts longer than Brand A.

2. _____ Brand C, Brand D, and Brand A all kept a sharp point.

3. _____ The eraser on Brand A did not last as long as the eraser on Brand C.

4. _____ The eraser worked well on all four brands.

5. _____ The lead did not keep a sharp point on one of the brands.

6. _____ Brand A did not work well in any of the areas.

7. _____ Brand C kept a sharp point, but it did not last one week.

8. _____ Brand D has an eraser that worked very well.

9. _____ Brand B would be a good choice if you wanted an eraser to last longer than one week.

10. Which pencil would you recommend that the class buy? _____

    Why? Use the information given in the chart to support your choice.

    _____

Read the chart. Then, answer the questions.

# Vertebrates

Vertebrates are animals with backbones. They can be sorted into different categories. This table shows the characteristics of five kinds of vertebrates.

| Class | Amphibian | Bird | Fish | Reptile | Mammal |
|---|---|---|---|---|---|
| Body covering | skin | feathers | scales | scales | skin and hair |
| Birth | egg | egg | egg | egg | live |
| Drinks mother's milk | no | no | no | no | yes |
| Warm- or cold-blooded | cold-blooded | warm-blooded | cold-blooded | cold-blooded | warm-blooded |
| Breathes with gills or lungs | gills when young, lungs when adult | lungs | gills | lungs | lungs |

1. Are amphibians warm- or cold-blooded? _____

2. Which kind of vertebrate drinks its mother's milk? _____

3. Which vertebrate breathes with gills its whole life?_____

4. What is the body covering of a bird? _____

5. Give two reasons why humans must be mammals._____

   _____

   _____

6. According to the chart, what do amphibians, fish, and reptiles have in common?

   _____

Read the passage. Then, answer the questions. Circle where you found the answer.

# Home Runs

In one year, two players broke a baseball record made 37 years earlier. In 1998, Sammy Sosa and Mark McGwire both beat the record for the greatest number of home runs in one baseball season. This record was originally held by Babe Ruth who had 60 home runs in 1927. Then, Roger Maris broke Ruth's record in 1961 with 61 home runs. Sammy Sosa, who played for the Chicago Cubs, had 66 home runs. Mark McGwire, who played for the St. Louis Cardinals, finished the season with 70 home runs.

For the entire 1998 season, fans watched the statistics to see which one of these players would first break the record made by Roger Maris. Once the record was broken by both players, it was a race to see who would hold the new record.

The table shows how many home runs Sammy Sosa and Mark McGwire made each month of the 1998 season.

| Player | March | April | May | June | July | August | September |
|--------|-------|-------|-----|------|------|--------|-----------|
| McGwire | 0 | 10 | 16 | 10 | 8 | 10 | 15 |
| Sosa | 0 | 6 | 7 | 20 | 9 | 13 | 11 |

1. Who first held the record for home runs in one season?_____

       text         chart        both

2. Who held the record at the end of 1961? _____

       text         chart        both

3. At the end of 1998, who held the record for home runs? _____

       text         chart        both

4. Who had the most home runs in June of 1998?_____

       text         chart        both

5. Which month did Sammy Sosa beat Roger Maris's record?_____

       text         chart        both

6. Did Mark McGwire beat the old record and gain the title in the same month or different months? Which month(s)?_____

       text         chart        both

Read the report. Then, answer the questions. Circle where you found the answer.

# Insect Report

Ivan presented a report about the importance of insects. He included information about how insects pollinate plants. He listed products we use that depend on insect pollination, such as cotton blue jeans, jack-o-lanterns, and apples. He told the class that in the last 10 years, we have lost about one-fourth of the insect pollinators. This is due to such things as wildflowers disappearing and pesticides being used. Ivan also displayed step-by-step directions with photos showing how to build a bumblebee house. Ivan wanted to know if his report could change how people felt about insects. He surveyed the class before and after his report. Here are the results of his surveys.

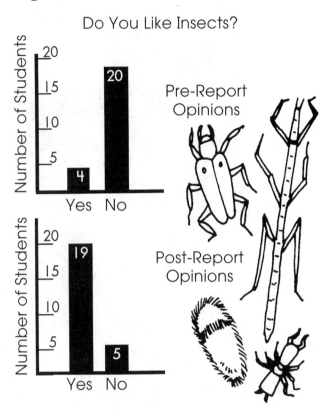

Do You Like Insects?

Pre-Report Opinions

Post-Report Opinions

1.  Do the students feel the same about insects before and after the report?

    _____

    text              graphs              both

2.  Why are insects important? _____

    text              graphs              both

3.  Compare the pre- and post-report graphs. Write two true statements about the graphs. Consider using words such as *most*, *fewer*, and *more than*.

    _____

    _____

    _____

4.  Highlight details in the report that may have caused the post-report opinions.

Read the table of contents. Then, answer the questions.

# Science Book

1. In which unit would you look if you wanted information about your inner ear? _____

2. If you were reading page 17, which could you be reading about?

   _____ the difference between a solid and a liquid

   _____ how a solid changes to a liquid

   Explain your choice. _____

   _____

   _____

3. If you want to know about diamonds, emeralds, coal, or sulfur, on what pages could you look?

   _____

**Science Book**

**Unit I Chemist**.................................. I
Chapter I States of Matter.................3
Chapter 2 Physical Changes ...........12
Chapter 3 Chemical Changes.........20

**Unit 2 Sound** .................................. **31**
Chapter I Vibrations........................33
Chapter 2 The Inner Ear...................46

**Unit 3 Rocks**.................................. **57**
Chapter I Rock Formations.............59
Chapter 2 Minerals...........................70
Chapter 3 Weathering.....................86

**Unit 4 Plants** .................................. **98**
Chapter I Plant Cycle ................... 100
Chapter 2 Environments................ 117

4. If you were reading page 109, which could you be reading about?

   _____ the types of plants that thrive in the rainforest

   _____ how a seed grows into a seedling, then a plant, which produces a seed

   Explain your choice. _____

5. If you are reading about how wind and water change rock formations, what unit and chapter are you reading?_____

Name_____

Read the diagram. Then, answer the questions.

# Family Tree

A family tree is a diagram that shows relationships in a family. A horizontal tie indicates two people who were married. A tie going down the page indicates a child. Look at the family tree of John and Sara. It shows four generations of their family.

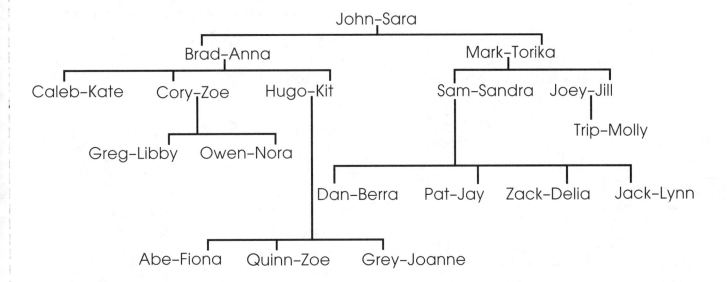

1.  How many children do Sam and Sandra have?_____

2.  Who is Fiona's husband? _____

    Who are Fiona's parents? _____

    Who are Fiona's grandparents?_____

    Who are Fiona's great-grandparents? _____

3.  Does the diagram give the name of the following:

    Lynn's husband?_____    Lynn's parents?_____    Lynn's children?_____

4.  What is the relationship between Zoe and Fiona?_____

5.  Name a married couple in the third generation who did not have children.

    _____ and _____

6.  Name two cousins. _____ and _____

# Answer Key

## Page 5

1. Warm, winter; Details: Ants dig deep into the ground. Beetles stack up in piles under rocks or dead leaves. Female grasshoppers die. Bees gather in a ball in the middle of their hive.

## Page 6

1. Pompeii before the Eruption: Pompeii was a rich and beautiful city in the Bay of Naples. It was close to a volcano named Mount Vesuvius. Pompeii during the Eruption: The sky in Pompeii was black, and ash rained down on it. The city was covered in over 12 feet of ash. Pompeii after the Eruption: The city is just as it was before the eruption.

## Page 7

1. C; 2. A; 3. B; 4. D

## Page 9

1. B; 2. D; 3. A; 4. father; uncle; 17; three; Kublai Khan; coal used as fuel; paper money instead of coins; papermaking and printing processes; 20

## Page 11

1. rocks; 2. C; 3. Topic Sentence: Rocks may be formed in three different ways. Subtopics: Igneous rocks are formed from extremely high temperatures. Sedimentary rock is formed when loose materials are pressed together over time. Metamorphic rocks are rocks that have been formed by some major change. Supporting Details: Magma is forced through cracks in the earth and, as it cools, it forms igneous rock. Lava comes to the surface of the earth and cools and forms igneous rock. Loose materials like sand, stone, and decomposed plants and animals gather on the bottom of the ocean. Water gets pressed out and these materials get cemented together to form sedimentary rock. Pressure and heat change metamorphic rocks. These processes may change the way the rock looks or even what it is made up of.

## Page 12

1. It, breakfast, Breakfast is important. Breakfast is an important meal. 2. It, computer, Computers can help you do many things. The computer is a helpful tool. 3. They, deer, Deer do not eat meat. Deer are herbivores.

## Page 13

1. Topic: Sharpening your pencil; Main Idea: how to always be prepared and have a sharpened pencil; Details: Good times to sharpen a pencil are before or after school and at recess. Keep an extra sharp pencil in your desk so you have a pencil at a time when you may not be able to use the sharpener. 2. Topic: Sleeping; Main Idea: Getting enough sleep is important to a child's health. Details: Sleep helps you stay focused on learning and allows you to think clearly. Most well-rested people get along better with others.

## Page 14

1. Austin, Texas; 2. bats; 3. Bats live under the bridge during the day because the sun does not shine under the bridge. The bats are Mexican free-tailed bats and there were over a million of them. The bats are gentle animals and do not attack people or cars. 4. bats; clouds; 5. Bats eat over 10,000 pounds of insects every night.

## Page 15

1. to persuade the reader to like bees; 2. Main Idea: Bees help to provide us with fruits, vegetables and other plants. Details: Bees help pollinate plants. If plants are not

# Answer Key

pollinated, seeds are not made. 3. Main Idea: Bees are in trouble. Details: A tiny mite is killing baby bees. Other bees are being killed by pesticides.

## Page 16
1. D; 2. C; 3. D; 4. C

## Page 17
1. C; 2. false; 3. step 3

## Page 18
1. aurora borealis; 2. 10 to 20 minutes; 3. on the sun; 4. the sun's atmosphere; 5. water from a hose that someone swings over their head; 6. a storm of particles hitting the atmosphere; 7. when the plasma particles stop striking

## Page 19
1. Topic Sentence: Many states border the five Great Lakes in the United States. Main Supporting Details: Michigan touches four of the Great Lakes. Wisconsin is a state that touches two Great Lakes. Illinois borders the southern part of Lake Michigan. Minor Supporting Details: Michigan supports many state parks that border the Great Lakes. Tourists visit and enjoy the water of Wisconsin in different ways. Visitors and people from Illinois enjoy the lake for swimming, boating, and viewing.

## Page 20
1. pepperoni, pineapple, olives; 2. yes, your favorite pizza toppings; 3. no; 4. 350°F (149°C), 10 minutes; 5. tomato sauce; 6. cheese; 7. Answers will vary.

## Page 21
1. Check students' drawings and highlighting.

## Page 23
1. weeds, mowing the lawn; weeds, seeing interesting insects and butterflies and adding them to his collection; 2. overgrown bushes, trimming the branches; a branch in front of a window, sneaking out of his room; holes in the screened porch, fixing the holes; the screened porch, making a fort; 3. Check students' drawings and highlighting.

## Page 25
1775: Paper money was first issued. 1785: US government decided the money system would be based on the dollar. 1860: US government issued paper money. 1865: Secret Service was established to control counterfeits. 1929: Bills were all made the same size. 1990: New security features were added to money to prevent counterfeiting. 1999: Only the 1-, 2-, 5-, 10-, 20-, 50-, and 100-dollar bills are still produced. 1. fake; 2. 1865; to stop counterfitting. 3. giving out; 4. The back of the money was printed with green ink. 5. George Washington, Abraham Lincoln, Thomas Jefferson; 6. 1929; 7. to prevent counterfeiting

## Page 27
1. to learn more about why they happen so they can warn people when the water is not safe; 2. relating to sea life; 3. nutrients, sunlight, and water; 4. irritate people's eyes, noses, and throats; people's lips and tongues tingle; people with asthma have a hard time breathing; 5. grow; 6. a dinoflagellate; 7. The weather is almost always warm, and many interesting plants and animals live in the water. 8. to look for seashells to collect because the poisons kill the animals in the shells and then the shells wash up on the beach; 9. stay away from the beach

# Answer Key

## Page 29
1. C; 2. 7; 3. 6; 4. one year; 5. B; 6. F, T, T; 7. not given; 8. not given; 9. not given; 10. Answers will vary.

## Page 30
1. index; 2. atlas; 3. glossary; 4. dictionary; 5. thesaurus; 6. atlas; 7. encyclopedia; 8. thesaurus; 9. index

## Page 31
1. hide, bone, fish; 2. B; 3. Answers will vary. Check students' summaries.

## Page 32
1. 2, 4, 3, 1; 2. do; 3. C; 4. You see new plants growing in places there were none the year before because the seeds traveled there either on an animal, a person, or the wind.

## Page 33
1. Find a place for everything and try to keep it in its place. 2. On Tuesdays, he cleans his desk. 3. When Daniel takes something out of his desk, he tries to put it back in its place. 4. When Daniel takes something out of his desk he tries to do it without making a mess. 5. Keeping your desk clean takes planning and time.

## Page 35
1. Name: Wilma Mankiller, Date Born: 1945, Tribe: Cherokee, Accomplishment: Improved health care, civil rights, and other important causes; Name: Crazy Horse, Date Born: 1849, Tribe: Lakota, Accomplishment: Kept the Native American way of life from disappearing; Name: Chief Joseph, Date Born: 1840, Tribe: Nez Percé, Accomplishment: Remained at peace with the military for his people; Name: Red Cloud, Date Born: 1822, Tribe: Lakota, Accomplishment: helped to hold and gain land for the Lakota people

## Page 36
1. A carapace is a shell. paragraph 2; 2. Horseshoes are related to spiders. paragraph 2; 3. A telson is a body part that looks like a tail. paragraph 3; 4. The horseshoe crab's tail is used to flip itself over. paragraph 3; 5. The horseshoe crab's blood is blue. paragraph 5; 6. Scientists use horseshoe crab blood to stop poisons. paragraph 7; 7. Scientists use horseshoe crabs' eyes for research. paragraph 6; 8. *Limulus Polyphemus* is the scientific name for a horseshoe crab. paragraph 1; 9. Horseshoe crabs eat clams, worms, and invertebrates. paragraph 2

## Page 38
1. Francis Scott Key wrote the words to "The Star-Spangled Banner." paragraph 1; 2. The song was written during The War of 1812. paragraph 1; 3. Francis Scott Key was a lawyer. paragraph 2; 4. James Madison was president when the song was written. paragraph 2; 5. Mr. Key was on a British warship when he wrote the song. paragraph 6; 6. The British were attacking Baltimore. paragraph 5; 7. The flag Mr. Key was watching was made by Mary Pickersgill and her daughter Caroline. paragraph 4; 8. The song's original name was "The Defense of Fort McHenry." paragraph 7

## Page 40
1. nursemaid; cleaner; guard; 2. one teaspoonful; 3. follows directions given by another bee; 4. 1, 3, 5, 4, 2

## Page 41
1. Florida: bordered by salt water; Sharks, jellyfish, and dolphins are found in these waters. Guests can find seashells on the shore. It is found in the south. It is warm all year round. Oranges and coconuts are

# Answer Key

grown here. Florida and Michigan: They are both peninsula states. They are both found in the United States. Michigan: It is bordered by freshwater lakes. Freshwater fish like salmon and trout are found in these waters. Guests love sandy beaches and sand dunes. It is found in the north. It has four seasons with great temperature ranges. Blueberries, apples, cherries, and peaches are grown here.

## Page 42

1. Carnival and Pond Life, Carnival and Pond Life, Carnival and Pond Life, Carnival;
2. Pond Life, boots or waders, so they can walk through the pond; 3. Pond Life; 4. They are both outside. 5. F, T, T, F.

## Page 43

1.

|  | Fahrenheit | Celsius |
|---|---|---|
| Invented by | Gabriel Fahrenheit | Anders Celsius |
| Water freezes | 32°F | 0°C |
| Normal body temperature | 98.6°F | 37°C |
| Water boils | 212°F | 100°C |

## Page 44

1. He was the first American to circle Earth.
2. He was the oldest astronaut ever to circle Earth. 3. went around

## Page 45

1962: 40 years old, first American to circle the earth, *Friendship 7*, only one, orbited three times, one window, no computers, talked to people; 1998: 77 years old, *Discovery*, six other astronauts, orbited 144 times, 10 windows to look out of; five computers; 1962 and 1998: orbited Earth, Scientists wanted to observe his reaction to the space environment. He was an American hero.

## Page 47

1. Underground Railroad: group of people helping slaves escape to freedom, Railroad Train: tracks, caboose, engine, Both: conductors, passengers, stations, moved people along

## Page 48

1. Cause: Most Americans were too busy building a country out of a wilderness to think about collecting coins. Cause: Large-sized cent coins became hard to get. Cause: Coin collecting became popular in the United States in the 1840s.

## Page 49

1. regular ice; 2. dry ice; 3. regular ice; 4. dry ice; 5. dry ice; 6. dry ice.

## Page 51

1. Check student's drawings; 2. Effect: The electricity was knocked out for the entire street. Cause: The electricity was knocked out. Effect: She jumped on the counter and landed on a cookie sheet in the dish rack. Cause: The marbles scattered all over the table and floor. Effect: The pan struck the flour container. Cause: The battery died and all went dark. Effect: He upset the marble jar. Cause: Kitty landed on the edge of the cookie sheet in the disk rack. Cause: Muttsie jumped at the noise of the marbles and ran toward Wayne's voice. Effect: Everything became covered in white. Cause: Mom heard all the noise.

## Page 52

1. The effect of Bonnie being born into a speed skating family was that her brothers and sisters always encouraged her.
2. Bonnie's brothers and sisters placed skates over her shoes because there weren't any skates small enough for her tiny feet. 3. The effect of Bonnie's practice and hard work

# Answer Key

was that she became the words best female speed skater.

## Page 53
1. D; 2. A; 3. B; 4. Water is evaporated from Earth. The air holds that water. Water then cools and forms a cloud.

## Page 54
Facts: Diamonds are crystals made of carbon. Diamonds are used to cut many hard materials. A diamond can only be cut by another diamond. The largest diamond weighed one and one-third pounds.
Opinions: Everyone knows diamonds are the most beautiful stones on Earth. It is worth the effort to find these beautiful jewels. Even small diamonds are something people enjoy more than any other jewel.

## Page 55
1. O; 2. F; 3. F; 4. O; 5. F; 6. O; 7. Answers will vary.

## Page 56
Opinion Words: pathetic, terrible, sad, beautiful, exciting, perfect, outstanding, difficult, dependable, awesome, fabulous, giant, impressive; 1. The Dogs' score was 12 at the end of the first quarter. Shaw scored four three-pointers in the final quarter. The Dogs and the Wild Ones played each other on Friday night. 2. The Mudpies and the Quicksanders played each other. The Quicksanders won the game 78 to 77. Gladd dunked the ball just before the buzzer went off. 3. The Kilometers beat the Miles 86 to 68. Dolby scored half of the Kilometers' points. Dolby is 6-feet-8-inches tall.

## Page 57
1. B; 2. D; 3. T, F, T, F

## Page 58
1. Opinion, hard, deserved; 2. Fact; 3. Fact;
4. Opinion, beautiful; 5. Fact; 6. Opinion, easy; 7. Fact; 8. Fact; 9. Fact; 10. Opinion: great; 11. Fact; 12. Fact; 13. Opinion, beautiful, hard; 14. Opinion, interesting; 15. Opinion, easy

## Page 59
1. A; 2. D; 3. Answers will vary but should include facts that describe the Milky Way galaxy. 4. Milky Way; 5. a star cluster

## Page 61
1. 5; 2. woodwinds; 3. woodwinds; 4. flutes; woodwinds; 5. clarinets; 6. horns; 7. violas; 8. horns

## Page 62
1. B; 2. A; 3. A, B, D; 4. Answers will vary but may include floods, destruction, and harm to people who have not taken shelter.

## Page 63
1. D; 2. B; 3. building plain wire fences, planting shrubs; 4. kept cattle from wandering onto railroad tracks

## Page 65
1. B; 2. D; 3. C; 4. A

## Page 67
1. to explain to readers the purpose of a commercial and to warn them of how commercials might influence them; 2. They can be entertaining and thought-provoking. 3. They can convince you of something that is not true. 4. the thought that you need something you might not really need; 5. power button; 6. Answers will vary. 7. Answers will vary.

## Page 68
1. D; 2. B; 3. Answers will vary.

## Page 69
1. Samantha, birthday; 2. Mother, The passage says, "I knew she would like the surprise from her father and me." 3. a sibling (brother or

# Answer Key

sister), The passage says, "Mom and Dad let me do extra chores to earn the money."

## Page 70
1. Ms. Wagner, She calls Jason's mom to solve the problem. 2. Jason. He forgot his lunch. 3. Jason's mom, She brings Jason's lunch to school.

## Page 71
1. good, She met her goal and she likes reading now. 2. Maddie did all the things she planned to do. 3. She read every day before school. She read every day after school. She paid attention when she read and made sure what she read made sense.

## Page 72
1. shopping, The author does not write a lot of details about this activity. 2. going to the pond, The author talks a lot about the fish in the pond and what they ate, also about the ducks and how the author fed them bread. 3. going to the caves, He says, "they were really cool" and talks a lot about what they looked like as well as what they had to wear in the caves.

## Page 73
1. The author enjoys cleaning the classroom. 2. right, She writes, "I told him he should have picked it up or told everyone he was going to take care of it later." 3. wrong, He said he wanted to show the teacher.

## Page 75
1. Good: eating take-out food, playing in the snow; Negative: being cold, having wet clothes; 2. He means that she got take-out food from a restaurant. The words that tell me that are when he says, "I hope she will pick up take-out food more often." 3. Good: go fishing, pick up shells; Negative: wearing sunscreen, being too hot

## Page 76
1. B; 2. C; 3. D; 4. C

## Page 77
1. A; 2. B; 3. B

## Page 79
1. B; 2. C; 3. his fingernails; 4. She is pregnant. She lives at the zoo. She likes bananas. 5. She might feel like her owners abandoned her.

## Page 81
1. A, C; 2. optimistic, possibly emotional; 3. Dozens of people were taken to area hospitals, and many houses were completely destroyed. 4. E, F; 5. Dorothy, Auntie Em, Uncle Henry, and Dorothy are all characters in *The Wizard of Oz*.

## Page 82
5; 1; 6; 4; 3; 2

## Page 83
1. chocolate; 2. It was very expensive. 3. expensive, The article says, "Making the milk chocolate took a lot of work and was very expensive." 4. make it in large amounts; 5. He mass produced milk chocolate and bars and sold it to people so that everyone could enjoy it. 6. no; The article says "as early as 1000 BC, people enjoyed chocolate in a drink." The article also says, "It wasn't until 1828 that a Dutch chemist found a way to make the fine powder we know as cocoa." 7. Answers will vary.

## Page 84
1. C; 2. A; 3. D; 4. A

## Page 85
1. Venus flytrap; 2. She went to the library to find out more about Venus flytraps. 3. The Venus flytrap is a carnivorous plant. 4. meat-eating; 5. Kayla will be sure to feed the Venus flytrap the appropriate food to

# Answer Key

keep it healthy and alive. Check students' highlighting.

## Page 86
1. D; 2. C; 3. A; 4. B

## Page 87
1. C; 2. C; 3. B; 4. books ,magazines, and menus

## Page 88
1. B; 2. C; 3. A; 4. C; 5. C

## Page 89
1. Ginny is a good gardener. 2. It was raining really hard. 3. The puppy made Patrick and Tara very tired. 4. Ruby just had to smile.

## Page 90
1. They would look for information everywhere. 2. Two people thinking together come up with better ideas than one person can by himself. 3. People don't behave as well when the person in charge is gone.

## Page 91
4. What someone else has always looks better. 5. Bill was in more trouble now than he had been to start with. 6. Rebecca must be honest with her teacher and accept the consequences.

## Page 92
1. From left to right:11, 12, 4, 10, 5, 2, 3, 13, 1, 15, 14, 8, 9, 7, 16, 6

## Page 93
1. A; 2. S; 3. S; 4. A; 5. S; 6. A; 7. S; 8. S; 9. A; 10. S

## Page 94
1. B; 2. C; 3. A; 4. B; 5. A

## Page 95
1. see; 2. whole; 3. soar; 4. weigh; 5. sun

## Page 97
1. A. S – divert; A – attract; B. S – change; A – let be; C. A – clumsy; S – graceful;

D. A – truth; S – trick; 2. The author means that the magician is getting the audience to focus somewhere else while doing a trick so the audience doesn't catch on to what is really happening. 3. sleight-of-hand; illusions; and escape magic; 4. A – F; B – T; C – T; D – F

## Page 98
1. D; 2. F; 3. H; 4. A; 5. G; 6. B; 7. C; 8. E

## Page 99
1. C; 2. all the facts about Elizabeth Cady Stanton; 3. Biographies, people, Biographies, people's lives

## Page 100
1. D; 2. the moral or lesson at the end of the story; 3. Fables, animals, Fables, teaching a lesson

## Page 101
1. ice; 2. a snowstorm; 3. kite; 4. the night; 5. mice; 6–8. Answers will vary.

## Page 102
1. D; 2. B; 3. Answers will vary.

## Page 103
1. A, has a great name; B, won the cup two years in a row at the Newmarket Races; C, had the sweetest temper; D, never kicked or bit; 2. has had a good upbringing and has manners; 3. A

## Page 105
1. C; 2. B; 3. Answers will vary. 4. D; 5. Answers will vary.

## Page 106
1. a dog; 2. no; 3. yes; 4. she does not like Ralph; because the passage says Ralph knew he would get swatted with the broom or sprayed with the hose like before, implying that he had done it before, and also because the lady screams and she sprays him with a hose; 5. Check students' drawings and highlighting.

# Answer Key

## Page 107

1. Winter; 2. Egyptian Desert; 3. Mother's Day; 4. Medieval England; 5. Ancient Rome

## Page 108

1. past; 2. present; 3. present; 4. future; 5. past; 6. present

## Page 109

1. in the morning; 2. outside in the springtime; 3. Heath and Shane; 4. Shane wants to skip school with Heath today and Heath doesn't think it is right. 5. Answers will vary but may include: Heath will not skip school because he knows that he will get in a lot of trouble at home if he does. Check students' highlighting.

## Page 110

1. early evening; 2. on the beach of an ocean; 3. Gabe and Hannah; 4. Gabe doesn't know what creature he has found or if it is going to hurt him. 5. Answers will vary but may include: Gabe will probably talk to Hannah's sister about horseshoe crabs since Hannah told him she knew a lot about them. Check students' highlighting.

## Page 111

1.

| Problem | Solution |
|---|---|
| The television is out and you cannot listen to the news for information about the storm. | A battery-powered radio will help you get weather and emergency information. |
| The well has stopped working so you cannot flush the toilet. | Fill empty milk jugs with fresh water. |
| The furnace will not start and it is getting very cold in the house. | Find extra blankets or purchase a generator with gasoline to run the furnace. |
| You are hungry and your electric stove doesn't work. | Keep healthy foods on hand that can be prepared and eaten without the use of electricity such as fruit, bread, and peanut butter. |
| The power is out and it is dark in the house. | Make sure you have a non-electrical light source, such as a flashlight, lantern, or candles. |

## Page 113

1. C; 2. A; 3. B; 4. B; 5. C

## Page 114

1. T; 2. F; 3. F; 4. F; 5. T; 6. F; 7. T; 8. F; 9. F; 10. Check students' answers and reasoning

## Page 115

1. cold-blooded; 2. mammal; 3. fish; 4. feathers; 5. because they are born live and have lungs; 6. come from an egg, don't drink their mother's milk, cold blooded

## Page 116

1. Babe Ruth, in the text; 2. Roger Maris, in the text; 3. Mark McGwire, in the chart; 4. Sammy Sosa, in the chart; 5. September, in the chart; 6. same month, September, in the chart

## Page 117

1. no, in the graphs; 2. for pollination, in the text; 3. Most students did not like insects before Ivan's report. Fewer than 5 students liked insects before the report. More than 15 (19) students liked insects after the report. 4. Check students' highlighting.

## Page 118

1. Unit 2 Sound; 2. how a solid changes to a liquid; because between pages 12 and 19, the book discusses physical changes and a physical change is the change between a solid and a liquid; 3. 70 through 85; 4. how

a seed grows into a seedling, then a plant, which produces a seed; because between pages 100 and 116, the book discusses the plant cycle, and the plant cycle includes how a seed grows into a seedling and then into a plant; 5. Unit 3, Chapter 3 Weathering

## Page 119

1. 4; 2. Abe, Hugo and Kit, Brad and Anna; John and Sara; 3. yes, yes, no; 4. sisters-in-law; 5. Caleb and Kate; 6. Answers will vary but may include Jay and Grey as one set of cousins.